INTEGRATING THE

URBAN SCHOOL

Integrating the Urban School

.63-22136

Proceedings of the Conference on Integration in the New York City Public Schools

Co-chairmen:	Gordon J. Klopf
	Teachers College, Columbia University
	Israel A. Laster
	American Jewish Committee New York Chapter
Convenor:	Mrs. Ethel Schwabacher
	Urban League of Greater New York
Program Chairman:	Harold Schiff
	Anti-Defamation League of B'nai B'rith New York Regional Office
Coordinator:	Bertrand Phillips
	Urban League of Greater New York

BUREAU OF PUBLICATIONS

TEACHERS COLLEGE, COLUMBIA UNIVERSITY

1963

iii

MANUFACTURED IN THE UNITED STATES OF AMERICA

Contents

Introduction

Integration in the New York City public schools has long been a concern of human relations agencies, institutions of higher education, and the New York City Board of Education. Individuals representing a number of agencies met in the late spring of 1963 to review the present situation, and they evolved a plan for conferences dealing with integration in the schools.

With the assistance of individuals from the Urban League of Greater New York, the American Jewish Committee, the Anti-Defamation League of B'nai B'rith, the New York City public schools, and Teachers College, Columbia University, a planning committee for the conferences was established. The committee invited a number of groups to be participating organizations in the conferences.

The goal of the proposed conferences was to formulate a concept of integration for the New York City schools. This concept was to include contributions from the behavioral sciences. There were to be recommendations on educational policies and processes for the school system and for those institutions preparing school personnel. There was also to be an exploration of the role of the community and its agencies in the shaping of policies for integration in the schools. Twenty participating organizations became the sponsors of the Conference, which was held at Teachers College, Columbia University, on May 1 and 2, 1963. Some 130 key community and education leaders were present. A follow-up Work Conference was held on June 14 at Bank Street College of Education. The planning committee arranged the two Conferences and edited the recommendations and findings.

The Proceedings consist of five papers presented at the Conference, a summary of the content of the Conference sessions, the recommendations and findings of both the Conference and the follow-up Work Conference, and readings from *The Fire Next Time,* by James Baldwin. The appendix includes a bibliography, a list of the participants and of the participating organizations, *Guiding Principles for Securing Racial Balance in Public Schools,* by James E. Allen, Jr., Commissioner of Education, State of New York, and a Statement of Policy by the New York City Board of Education.

The findings do not necessarily imply that all of the organization participants approved the suggested resolutions and recommendations. The participants present at the Work Conference arrived at a general consensus on the spirit and principle underlying a concept of integration for the New York City public schools. There were individual differences of opinion expressed on some of the recommendations. The Conference Proceedings should serve as a blueprint for action for the Board of Education in co-operation with citizens and community organizations in achieving integration in the New York City public schools.

A great many individuals worked on the planning of the actual production of the Conference. Most of these are listed as either committee members or Conference participants. Individuals who served as office staff members of the co-operating organizations and as volunteers who deserve appreciation and recognition for their contributions are:

James Morrison, Esther Clay, R. Abby Nachman, Robert Davis, Raphael Hendrix, Edith Marquez, Vera Kristeller, Joyce Patton, Thomas Bratter, Kenneth King, and Marguerite Manning.

A special word of appreciation must be given to Bertrand Phillips, Conference Co-ordinator, whose knowledge of the subject, industry and contribution, and organization and administrative skill helped the Conference to achieve its goal.

New York   GORDON KLOPF
September 1963   ISRAEL LASTER

INTEGRATING THE

URBAN SCHOOL

I

Papers and Summary

Our Wasted Potential

Daniel C. Thompson
Professor of Sociology
Howard University

Introduction

Ours is an awe-inspiring age. We contemplate the future of mankind generally, and the future of our own society specifically, with mingled optimism and fear. On the one hand, man's eternal desire to build a better world, to reconstruct society in such a way that ignorance, poverty, diseases, inequalities, fears and wars will either be eliminated or greatly reduced, offers—at long last—some real hope of fulfillment. On the other hand, our capability for destruction, for actually wiping out civilization as we know it, is infinitely greater, and even more disquietingly probable, than at any other time in history.

I am convinced that in the final analysis, whether mankind proceeds in the direction of creative social reconstruction or international destruction, whether our own nation continues to grow stronger and more significant as the leader of the free world, or declines in strength and ceases to be a symbol of freedom and democracy will be determined in very large part, not just by our

1

economic and military strength, but the degree to which we find ways of developing our most basic resource—our human potential. Pointedly, the true greatness of this nation, or any nation, will be determined in the future (even now) by the level of its education, skills, scientific know-how, morale and the general character of its citizens, as well as by its military strength.

Indeed, Arnold J. Toynbee, the noted British scholar, concluded after a long and exhaustive analysis of world history, that practically all of the fallen civilizations of the past—such as ancient Egypt, Rome, Babylon, Greece, and Syria—began to decline, and most of them actually fell during their most economically prosperous period, when their armies were larger and better equipped than ever before in their nation's history. Why, then, did these great civilizations decline, fall and finally disappear as such? Toynbee suggests the answer: These great nations allowed their youth to become defiled—or they failed to pass on to their youth the high ideals, the basic values, the fundamental skills, and the nobility of purpose which, in the first place, brought their nations to greatness. Thus the lesson of history is this: Our nation will begin to decline in strength and nobility of purpose, and could eventually fall, unless we take care to conserve and develop our most precious, and altogether indispensable, resource—*the youth of this nation.*

On this point President John F. Kennedy says that

Our progress as a nation can be no swifter than our progress in education. Our requirements for world leadership, our hopes for economic growth, and the demands of citizenship itself in an era such as this all require the maximum development of every young American's capacity. The human mind is our fundamental resource.

With this warning in mind we should become fully aware that the wide gap between the academic achievements of certain culturally deprived groups in our cities, particularly Negro youth and the average American child, is a national problem of the first magnitude. It indicates a tragic waste of talents and abilities which we simply cannot afford because our national greatness and international leadership depend ultimately upon the general quality of our population, upon the developed potential of each individual citizen.

We are already beginning to see how unwise it is to allow the great potential among our Negro youth to lay fallow, undeveloped, and unused. In practically every large city in the United States— especially in the large northern metropolises such as New York— problems stemming from widespread frustration and social disorganization on the part of Negroes are threatening not only to destroy the hopes as well as the talents of the masses of Negroes, themselves, but the very economic, social, and moral foundation of our society.

Symptoms of this gradual but steady decay in the system of values that undergirds American society are now so obvious that they can no longer be ignored or discounted. Among the most easily recognized symptoms are the steadily increasing rate of delinquency, crime, illegitimacy, drop-outs, unemployment, and general unrest upon our youth. As high as these rates are among Americans on the whole, they are up to five times as high among Negroes.

The Problem

In order to get a functional understanding of the nature and extent of the wasted talents among Negro youth it is necessary, first of all, to take into account three basic social facts:

(1) All human behavior is fundamentally normal behavior in the sense that it is learned. This is so whether a given pattern of behavior is regarded as socially reprehensible or socially approved. The basic motivations to learn or participate in a given pattern of behavior are the desire for security, the desire for recognition, the desire for new experience, and the desire for response.[1] Therefore, what is regarded generally as socially deviant behavior is basically a reflection of defects in education, or more broadly, in the process of socialization, whereby the child has not been brought to accept certain important norms and values which prevail in society as a whole; or he has come to internalize certain antisocial norms and values peculiar to some given social world or class of which he is a part. In other words, the child will tend to use the rules, techniques, and methods accepted by his reference group

---

[1] W. I. Thomas, *The Unadjusted Girl,* (Boston: Little, Brown and Co., 1928), pp. 1-40.

(a group or social world to which he either belongs or desires to belong) in his attempts to satisfy the basic desires just mentioned.

(2) No matter how social class may be defined—whether in terms of wealth, education, style of life, occupation, or aspiration —approximately 70 to 80 per cent of the Negro population in large northern cities are lower class.

Generally speaking, lower class parents are far too busy with the exigencies of day-to-day living to give much creative thought to long-range planning for their children. Thus during the past few years I have done several studies that revealed the vast wasted potential among Negro youth, particularly boys.[2] The following are characteristics of the Negro homes from which come the great majority of drop-outs, delinquents and unemployed youth:

(a) In about half of the homes one or both parents had a history of alcoholism, criminality, poverty, and instability.

(b) Practically all of the homes may be described as *culturally* impoverished. As a rule neither parent (or guardian) had received as much as a high school education. Furthermore, there was seldom any reading material found in their homes except the elementary school books used by the children.

In most homes there was a television or radio set, and sometimes a record player, yet members of the family had no manifest interest in any form of music and drama except that which might be classified as "low brow." Seldom did any member of the family listen attentively to news broadcasts or other types of informational programs.

(c) The houses, like the neighborhoods, in which they lived were generally ugly. There was seldom any effort to make surroundings beautiful with flowers, pictures or furnishings, and there were very few homes that had a spare room where the children could study quietly.

[2] Daniel C. Thompson, "A Profile of Social Classes in the Negro Community," *Proceedings of the Louisiana Academy of Sciences* (1956); *The Eighth Generation* (New York: Harper and Bros., 1960); "The Changing Status of Negroes in New Orleans," *The Journal of Social Science Teachers* (May, 1957); "The Social History of a Religious Cult," M. A. thesis; "Social Class Factors in Public School Education as Related to Desegregation," *American Journal of Orthopsychiatry* (July, 1956); "The Formation of Social Attitudes," *American Journal of Orthopsychiatry* (January, 1962).

(d) About a fourth of the children were born out of wedlock. Some parents were quick to admit that their children were unwanted.

(e) There was little evidence of family pride.

(f) Half of the homes were without a male head. Even when the father was present, the mother appeared to be the dominant figure.

(g) Parents had made no definite plans for their children's future. None, for example, had education policies to insure their children's schooling.

(h) By and large parents did not teach their children self-respect. More often the child was depreciated and derogated.

(i) Children had not been taught to aspire for more than day-to-day success. For instance, only occasionally did a drop-out or delinquent express any future occupational aspiration at all. When pressed to state some occupational aspiration they would casually name some "low-aspiration" occupation.

(j) The "problem" children had no clear conception of success as defined in traditional American thought. None identified with a great legendary or real hero in history. Actually the parents had never told these children traditional bedtime stories which function to delineate acceptable heroes or heroines.

(k) Case histories of most of these families revealed a series of traumatic stresses, strains and breakups brought on by chronic illness, imprisonment, poverty and/or separations.

(l) There was ample validation of the fact of the old proverb: "The apple does not fall far from the tree." That is, the several studies underscored the fact that children are not often very different from their parents.

Finally, among lower class Negroes there are at least four distinct social worlds: (1) the matriarchy, where the fact of being *female* is given great emphasis and *maleness* is a symbol of distrust, disrespect, and dishonor; (2) the gang, where *maleness* is defined in terms of aggressiveness, physical prowess, and the necessity to "prove yourself a man." Boys from matriarchial homes learn early to disrespect women—actually to reject any value associated with femaleness. Thus from the very start two large segments of Negro mass society are set against one another: Girls born and reared in matriarchial homes tend to distrust men and reject values identified with the "male principle" in society. Boys find various ways to demonstrate their rejection of the "female principle." In a sense, then, girls and boys reared in matriarchial homes become "natural enemies." This fact is basic in mapping out an approach to effective education. (3) Marginality, where children have shifted from one place to another, from one family to another and from one self-identity to another so often they have not had time to develop a stable self-identity. This confusion is reflected whenever they must make any decision, including school, courtship, or employment. (4) The nuclear family, where family members are tightly banded together, as it were, for protection against the outside world. Children from these homes tend to be suspicious, even of those who try to help them. In a sense, however, it is one of the most wholesome social worlds for the psychological development of children because there is considerable family pride, stability, and, more or less, clear self-identity.

Any program of compensatory education must take into account the fact that lower class Negro children suffer from different kinds of deprivations. Some need to develop wholesome attitudes regarding sex statuses and roles, some need to achieve stable self-identities, and others need to be taught that the world can be friendly, not just hostile. Most need to be made to feel that they are accepted as worthy participants in the middle-class-oriented schools to which they may be assigned.

(3) A third basic fact to be considered is that social structure in white society is the reverse of that in Negro society. That is, from 70 to 80 per cent of the white urban population may be classified as middle and upper class. This means that American culture generally, and schools in particular, are middle-class oriented. They lay great emphasis upon such values as self-respect, achieved social status and recognition, higher education, occupational success, stable family life, the willingness to sacrifice the satisfaction of immediate desires for long-range goals, hard work, and morality.

Now, let us again define our basic problem. It seems to be this: *How can we successfully and effectively integrate socially, culturally, and psychologically deprived Negro children into the best schools of our nation so that they might be prepared to participate in the main stream of our American culture?*

Before this question can be constructively answered it is necessary to take a much closer look at the nature of the lower class Negro masses, such as can be found in New York City. This requires, at least, a brief examination of their rural cultural background and their ghetto society.

Rural Cultural Background

At the close of the Civil War about 90 per cent of the Negroes lived in the rural South. Today this has changed—about 40 per cent, or eight million or so, live outside the South. Thus, for instance, during the last two decades the Negro population in New York City has increased nearly two and a half times, and now numbers over a million and constitutes at least fourteen per cent of the total population. Furthermore, a steady stream of Negro migrants is still flowing out of the South to this and other cities of the North and West.

At the close of World War II the danger of the wide educational gap between the masses of Negro children and the average white child became glaringly apparent. A few of this nation's leaders more or less mildly suggested that we could hardly afford to continue to waste the great potential in the Negro race as had been done over the years. Eventually Congress was asked to appropriate federal money to equalize educational opportunities throughout the nation. Ironically, the very states that would have benefitted most from such a program (the southern states) led the vicious fight to defeat this proposal because it would have included their Negro citizens. Many shortsighted northern congressmen could always be depended upon to join with their southern colleagues in defeating any attempt to equalize educational opportunities in the southern states. Therefore, gross inequalities in the educational opportunities for Negro youth in the South were allowed to remain.

The Negro Ghetto

Frustrated and discouraged Negroes left southern communities in search of better conditions, including better education for their children. For the most part they settled in segregated northern slums. Steadily these slums became bigger and bigger and more and more withdrawn from the main stream of the city's culture, and what was once a southern problem has now become the problem of New York City.

Gradually the Negro ghetto became increasingly like some of the culturally deprived communities from which the Negroes had migrated. The schools they found in Northern cities were, in some respects, very much better than the ones they left but not nearly good enough to equip them for the greater competition they encountered in these cities.

Some parents became completely dissatisfied and demanded the right to send their children to the higher standard schools attended by white children. Thus in 1958, in the Skipworth case, the Court agreed that Negro parents were in their rights to insist that their children should attend the best public schools available. Therefore, New York can no longer contain the problem of Negro education in a given area of the city. *It is no longer the problem of educating Harlem Negroes—but culturally deprived New Yorkers of all races.*

How the Problem of Cultural Deprivation Might Be Solved

Many New Yorkers described the Negro youngsters who transferred to formerly all white, or predominantly white, schools as "invaders." They seemed unable to comprehend that a child born in the rural areas of Mississippi is an American with the same rights as other Americans—that he has as much right to attend any school in New York City as does a child born in the most economically advantaged communities of this city. Therefore, the wiser New Yorkers did not define these Negro children as invaders —but as a "problem." Consequently, some noteworthy attempts have been made to bridge, or close, the scholastic gap between the culturally deprived and the more culturally fortunate in the schools of New York. I am certain, however, as much success as certain of these programs have had (particularly the imaginative Higher Horizons Program), you would agree with me that the problem is very far from being solved.

There are at least three possible approaches to the desegregation of schools:

(1) *The track program.* According to this program children are divided into three groups in terms of achievement. Those in

the highest track are prepared for higher education; those in the middle track for certain white-collar and skilled pursuits where average talents are needed, and those in the lowest track are encouraged to prepare for certain manual jobs.

Though refusing to take a stand on the merit of the track system, Conant[3] does say "I submit that in a heavily urbanized and industralized free society the educational experiences of youth should fit their subsequent employment."

There are at least two fallacies in this reasoning: one, experience has proven that it is extremely dangerous (even when we use the most advanced tests) to predict the future capabilities of a child ten or twelve years of age. With expert training some children whose I. Q.'s were apparently well below average, and whose motivation was very weak, showed great improvements in both and proved to be capable of qualifying for almost any occupation in our society.

Two, to prepare a child for some specific occupation he is supposed to pursue twenty or thirty years in the future, requires an impossible prognosis. In this rapidly changing technological society no one can say what old occupations will remain and what new occupations will be created.

(2) A second approach to desegregation is that of having what amounts to *three types of schools*. In this way the so-called "mentally superior" will be recruited from all segments of society just as will those of "average" and "below average" mentality, each group having its own specialized school.

Here again, an undemocratic decision must be made. It is true that a competent scientist or professor must have at least average mentality, yet the truth remains that society is not built by the mentally superior only, and there is in practically everyone hidden potential that may blossom with nurture. Furthermore, some of our most prolific "geniuses" have developed in the same schools with fellow students of just average abilities.

(3) *Democratic education.* The fundamental philosophy undergirding public school education in this country is that every American child should have the *same* educational opportunity as

[3] James B. Conant, *Slums and Suburbs,* (New York: McGraw-Hill Book Co., Inc., 1961), p. 40.

every other child. That is, in the competition for an education and for the rewards it may bring, *each individual child has the same right as every other child to succeed or fail.*

It may be that we are so scientifically advanced that we can save the child from needless academic failure. *I don't think so.* I don't think that we have had nearly enough experiments in democratic education to abandon it just yet. We need to continue to experiment in our efforts to make equal education available to all of our youth.

In order to provide the culturally deprived child with an equal democratic education I propose the following general approach:

(1) Our government on all levels (federal, state and local) will need to appropriate considerably more money for education than is now being done. As I see it we will need to spend something like twice the proportion of our tax money for the education of the culturally deprived as we do for those who are culturally fortunate. Therefore, our school systems would need to adopt flexible policies regarding educational experimentation.

(2) Foundations would need to bear most of the cost of experimentation and research. They would need to concentrate much of their funds, also, in the training of teachers specialized in dealing with the culturally deprived. *The most promising way of closing the cultural gap between the lower class Negro youth and the predominantly middle class white youth is superior teaching.*

Negro colleges are peculiarly equipped to provide the quality of teachers needed for the compensatory education Negro migrant children need. If foundations would provide funds whereby two or three per cent of the Negro and white college students could be carefully selected and intensely trained in these colleges under the personal supervision of professors who are, themselves, well-trained in Negro history and culture, it would be possible to produce a large number of teachers who are able to provide culturally deprived children with the insightful guidance and instruction they must have in order to develop their potentialities.

These specially trained teachers could solve two critical personnel problems: the flight of good teachers from predominantly Negro schools, and the acute shortage of male teachers.

As I see it college juniors would be selected for this program. They would be provided full college expenses and an additional year of graduate training especially structured to prepare them for the teaching of the culturally deprived. When they qualify for the program they would be paid considerably higher salaries than other teachers and given special social recognition. (The differential pay would be justified on the basis of their superior training in a specialized area of education.)

(3) Total community involvement is needed. It is my belief that when the government and foundations attempt to shoulder the total burden of educational improvement, most of their effort will be wasted. There must be generated a community-wide concern. All organizations and individuals in the community should be drawn into the program of integration and cultural uplift. This means that such a program will be well thought out so that specific, detail functions and tasks can be precisely assigned. When the individuals and organizations know precisely what is expected of them they can be expected to cooperate. Also they must be able to see exactly why their small or large contribution is essential to the success of the total operation. In this way hitherto untapped community resources can be channeled into an all-out educational program.

Finally, if we would save and develop the vast wasted talents and abilities among our culturally deprived youth, government on all levels, philanthropic foundations, talented individuals, and all organizations in the respective communities must pool their resources in a unified effort to bridge the cultural gap between these youth and others who have been socialized in superior middle-class homes and neighborhoods.

year of graduate training especially structured to prepare them for the teaching of the culturally deprived. When they qualify for the program they would be paid considerably higher salaries than other teachers and given special social recognition. (The differential pay would be justified on the basis of their superior training in a specialized area of education.)

(3) Total community involvement is needed. It is my belief that when the government and foundations attempt to shoulder the total burden of educational improvement, most of their effort will be wasted. There must be generated a community-wide concern. All organizations and individuals in the community should be drawn into the program of integration and cultural uplift. This means that such a program will be well thought out so that specific detail functions will then can be precisely assigned. When the individuals and organizations know precisely what is expected of them they can be expected to cooperate. Also they must be able to see exactly why their small or large contribution is essential to the success of the total enterprise. In this way hitherto untapped community resources can be channeled into an all-out educational program.

Finally, if we would save and develop the vast wasted talents and abilities among our culturally deprived youth, government on all levels, philanthropic foundations, talented individuals, and all organizations in the respective communities must pool their resources in a united effort to bridge the cultural gap between these youth and others who have been so neglected in superior middle-class homes and neighborhoods.

The Process of Integration

Melvin Tumin
Professor of Sociology and Anthropology
Princeton University

The schools of the United States are the single most important agents in the formation of our national character, in the shaping of our individual and collective futures, and in the creation of the tone and content of our interpersonal and intergroup relations. It is no accident that the greatest public debate our country has ever witnessed is now being conducted precisely with regard to the schools, a debate that raises to public dispute virtually every aspect of school structure and function. The consequences of education are such that it is possible to identify directly and immediately with the most intimate and personal effects upon us and our children, as well as to see clearly how everything that goes on in the schools affects our block, our neighborhood, our district, our city, our state, and our country.

Indeed, much of the shape of the rest of the world depends upon the outcomes of our educational debate and the forms our schools take. For in the best and most direct senses of the words, we as a nation are now conducting a crucial experiment, aimed at determining whether it is possible to produce a viable, respectworthy, free public school system available to everyone, regardless of origin and background, on the basis of citizenship. In this experiment we take as a fundamental premise that whatever the difficulties or temporary national emergencies, we owe every single young person in our country the right to *equal, equally good,* and *equally enduring* education. That premise is indispensable to our vision and view of ourselves as a democratic society. The achievement of that vision is indispensable to the maintenance and growth of a genuinely democratic society in which equal opportunity is a meaningful theme of action and not merely a solemn empty pledge. And, if we, the wealthiest, best educated, most committed-to-

13

democracy nation of the world cannot successfully win such an experiment, who can? It is in that crucial sense that much of the fate of the rest of the world for the perceivable future hinges importantly on what we here in this country do in the next several decades.

The crucial premise in this theme of democratic education is the premise of equal, equally good, and equally enduring education for all. Anything short of that is something less than equal opportunity. Moreover, anything short of that is hardly worth striving for, since we have excellent examples from all over the world of how to run elite or quasi-elite systems of education. These are easy, familiar, surefooted. But they aren't democratic and don't mean to be, and they are not envisioned as the groundwork of social systems of equal opportunity.

All the terrible travail we endure in this current period, as we go ahead with our experiment, arises from the strain between traditional themes and comfortable histories of special privileges and opportunities for selected segments of the population, on the one hand, and the newer, challenging, terribly difficult to realize theme of equal privileges and opportunities for all. The latter is so relatively new—at least in any form of concrete practice—and it so upsets existing sets of special privileges, and entails so much fumbling and experimenting, without any certain guarantees of success, that it is no wonder that so many of us find it difficult to rise to the conception of what is entailed for us, what we must be willing to do if it is to work, what traditional values must be displaced, what new forms of social relationships are demanded from all personnel connected with the schools and communities—children, parents, teachers, principals, superintendents, and others.

In this regard, however, in the regard of the difficulties we find in implementing the new equal opportunity theme, the schools are not much different from our families, our government, and the rest of our institutions. For, in more than a rhetorical sense of the word, this is an age of new freedoms and equalities: new equality for women and children who are for the first time in our history beginning to be treated as equals; new freedoms and rights for emerging nations and peoples throughout the world. New freedoms always disturb old privileges, old habits, old comforts and hence are likely to be resisted very strongly. But that is only as it must be.

We shall not accomplish anything significant in the field of education, nor in the fields of family life or international relations, without much struggle and conflict. We can hope to minimize the *destructive* aspects of such conflict. But we cannot hope for smooth, tranquil, easygoing transitions from one system to a sharply contrasting system. It seems to me we must accept the likelihood of a high level of dispute and conflict as a natural correlative of the process of change toward the democratic goals we commonly avow as worthy and worthwhile of achievement.

If I take what seems to be much time to lay in this background for our discussion this afternoon, it is because the full implications of equal education are not well and widely understood, and when they are understood they are clearly sensed as dangers by many persons who have enjoyed or hope to enjoy certain special privileged places in our as yet very unequal social structure. And we cannot proceed an inch in the process of integration unless we are quite clear that it means, sooner rather than later, equal education for all, and that that probably entails a great deal of disruption and social upset.

Equal education can and does mean only one thing: It means that every child must be taught in such a way that his potentialities for acquiring the facts, the insights, the understandings, the skills, the values, the perspectives, and the command over himself and his culture that we commonly agree are desirable shall have an equal chance of being developed.

There are clearly *three phases* or areas of validation of this notion of potentialities.

There is first the *freeing* of the potentialities so that they are available and not hidden, so that they are visible and identifiable. This in turn simply means that preschool experience, and the total social living context of the school child that bear down relevantly upon his potentialities, must be of the highest concern for the educator who is genuinely committed to equal education. I do not see how it is possible, therefore, to say that social engineering is not the concern of the school system. If the capacity of the child to learn what the schools have to offer is importantly determined by the interaction between the child and his nonschool environment— his home, his neighborhood, his class and ethnic group status, it is mindless and dangerous to think that one can wish away the significance of these nonschool factors by calling them social engineering and declaring they are not the responsibility or the proper domain of attention and concern of the school system. We care terribly much in the schools, as we should, about the child's physical health and physical readiness to take on the school routines and activities. We even care about his psychological health to the extent of trying, albeit not very successfully, to screen for mental health treatment where it seems required. On what conceivable grounds, then, can it be said that we cannot, within the schools, care about and attempt to do something about the *more general* conditions of psychological readiness to learn?

One may, of course, out of a desperate sense of the enormity of the tasks confronting us, try to cut our problems down to immediately manageable size by deliberately excluding from the focus of our attention such factors as seem to be somewhat less directly connected with the educational process. But if we do this we ought to recognize two things: (1) that we are thereby ensuring the continuity of some of the most serious problems we will face in the school, and (2), as a result, our horizons of what is possible in the actual classroom itself must be seriously reduced.

It is utterly wrong, therefore, to declare that as long as segregation is not intentional, we had better accept it and concentrate on improving the segregated schools. When the Supreme Court declared that segregated schools were inherently unequal, it said a lot more than perhaps it intended, and said correctly. For there can be no doubt that, in general, and on the average—without concern for individual exceptions to the contrary—all-Negro or predominantly Negro schools will remain inferior precisely because they are all Negro or predominantly Negro. It does not matter how much money one pours into such schools. It would not matter if one deliberately secured the cream of the teaching staff from all schools and put them all into the Negro schools. None of these would matter much, simply because to maintain a school as all or predominantly Negro, is to communicate vividly every day and every moment to the Negro children—no matter who else didn't get the message—that they are second class, inferior people.

I would not be very impressed at all even if one could convincingly demonstrate that national achievement norms on standardized tests had been exceeded by specially trained Negro populations. This education would still be inferior. By their very segregation they are being powerfully educated every moment of their segregated school existence into an identity as an undesirable, inferior group of people. And in this context the greater psychological comfort that some Negro children may experience when in segregated schools, as against the initial or even enduring discomfort when in situations of desegregation, is of little or no relevance. I do not mean to be mindless and heartless about the psychological costs. I will look at them in detail in a moment. But I am saying that appeals to the comfort of Negro children, to the freedom from artificial mixing, by whatever technique, have nothing whatsoever to comment about whether segregated schools are or are not inferior—and, if one may venture the words, undemocratic, unjustifiable, and, in even more demonstrable ways, harmful to both Negro and White beyond any other justification.

Typically, minority groups find comfort and refuge from a real or imagined hostile outside majority by ghettoizing themselves, if they are not deliberately ghettoized, into communities of persons like themselves where they do not have to read demeaning messages on the faces of their social partners all day long. But we all know that this is simply a vicious circle. There is no way out of the circle except to deghettoize the ghettos, to break down the ghetto walls, and to make free circulation of all people possible. There is no way of getting to comfortable free circulation of people except by starting with what are obviously the first efforts, which are almost always terribly uncomfortable and distressing for everyone concerned. People cannot come to learn to live well and peacefully and productively side by side until they have lived side by side for some time. There is no way of making a magical leap from a condition of isolation, ghettoization and all the mutual distrust implied into free and easy going peaceful neighborly relations. There is no way to integration except through desegregation.

I make these observations apropos the claim that the neighborhood, housing, and employment situations of school children and their parents are matters of social engineering not to be wrestled with by the schools. But the inescapable fact is that housing, neighborhoods, and jobs directly affect the availability and visibility of the school child's potentials for learning. Those are the factors, along with their correlatives in support, horizons, home aid, ambitions, self-images, and senses of alienation from societal responsibilities, that set basic inequalities in school-readiness into motion and keep them in motion in a circle of multiplying effects throughout the child's school career. If, then, in the first phase of factors affecting equal education, we set such inequalities into motion, we cannot hope seriously to reduce them or produce equality of education later unless we backtrack and attend to this first phase.

Learning difficulties and low levels of achievement are the symptoms. Low horizons of hope and aspiration, impairment of learning faculties, withdrawal from normal social involvements, these are the diseases. And the causes of those diseases are undoubtedly to be found in the larger social system of anti-Negro prejudice and discrimination, as these operate through and are manifested by segregated neighborhoods, low-paid jobs, high rates of unemployment, social exclusions, and all the other aspects of the system of segregation and discrimination with which we are so painfully familiar.

Whatever we may hope to be able to accomplish in the second and third phases of equal education, we cannot realistically set very high hopes at all if we start out with populations that are fundamentally and deeply unequal in their readiness to receive, be affected by, and profit from the things we do in the second and third phases. Social engineering designed to get at the sources of unequal readiness in the preschool experiences and the general social environments of our children are therefore of the highest order of educational relevance.

The second phase of equal education has to do with the formal school experience itself. Here there is more than curriculum; more than homogenous or heterogenous groupings; more than grades and examinations. Here we cannot avoid the impact, the terribly significant impact, of teacher's sensitivities, sensibilities, attitudes, and behavior. In the same vein, we must be aware of the crucial role played by principals and other supervisory personnel in the shaping of these attitudes and behavior. Here, too, we find the great impact of the attitudes and behavior of other school children with whom the so-called less-privileged children interact. There is no doubt whatsoever that the right kind of teacher and principal make the right kind of difference, the wrong kind of teacher and principal make the wrong kind of difference. The teacher sets the tone of social relationships in the classroom. She validates notions of good and bad. She determines what is to be rewarded and what punished. She certifies the rightness or wrongness of reacting to errors or so-called bad manners, or day dreaming, or withdrawal in one or another way. In short, the teacher, and behind her and with her the principal, determine what the general reactions will be of the more-privileged to the less-privileged school children, as these differences in privileges and backgrounds reflect themselves in the behavior and formal performances of the different children.

The teacher is the living model of right behavior. She is the moral guardian of democratic rights. She is the exemplary of understanding and sympathetic concern for the equal education of all children. She is either these or their opposites or some bad compromises with these basic elements of equal education. I say this full well aware that because the first-phase experiences of children are so uneven in so many cases, the teacher is often forced to deal, and often under impossible circumstances, with children whose potentialities are already well hidden, whose abilities are already substantially impaired, and whose attitudes are in the process of rapidly becoming inimical to adequate school performance. But it is impossible to take any position other than that *some* influence for the good, *some* change in the direction of desirable goals, can be effected by the teacher, however hardened the human materials in front of her, however impossibly difficult her classroom situation.

Here, then, teacher training and principal training become of the highest order of relevance. But certain over-all school policies are also crucial, and without them the best teacher cannot hope to function well. Let me try to say how these relate. For the teacher, the primary and indispensable requisites are (1) ability sensitively to perceive the human material in front of her, with all its fears, hopes, timidities, hostilities, sense of degradation, prides, and capacities; (2) an overriding concern that that child, with all of his or her special qualities, shall be made to feel free to learn and desirous to learn to the maximum available at that moment's level of readiness; (3) a capacity, which can be and has been learned by many teachers, to adapt curriculum materials to the particular quality and level of readiness the child exhibits at the given moment, and to alter, flexibly, upwards, downwards, sideways, those materials, as the child's attitudes and capacities vary and change from day to day.

But these things the teacher cannot hope to do, cannot even begin to dream of accomplishing, no matter how well trained he or she may be, unless there are fundamental structural supports from the general school policy.

I see here as indispensable in moving toward equal education for underprivileged children the following things:

(1) The elimination of competitive grading and graded curriculum and the substitution of the ungraded curriculum. The formal structures of the graded curriculum are an educational abomination. What in the world is the psychological or social significance or the educational value of such things as first grade, first semester, first marking period, or of A, B, C, D, etc.? They have nothing to do with the educational process or the development process at all.

Children do not grow or learn in units of semesters or quarters, and their abilities and performances bear no discernible relationship to such things as scores. Children learn what they are ready to learn, and able to learn. When they learn that much, they are ready to go on. There is no way out of this or around this basic fact. You either understand an arithmetic problem and how to solve it or you don't. The idea that you know 70 or 80 per cent of how to solve a problem is a nightmare. If you don't know how to solve a problem, you don't know how to solve it. And if you know how to solve it only 70 per cent of the time, then, if you are passed on to the more difficult problems, you are sure to learn how to solve them only 60 or 50 or 40 per cent of the time. And you don't become ready by January or June or September. You become ready to go on when you are ready to go on. To insist that you must make decisions in January and June as to who will go and who will not leads to such abominations as failing substantial numbers of children at artificial moments and by artificial standards, and, in any event, it introduces the concept of failure into the educational process, when again that concept simply has no relevance, except perhaps at the highest level of professional training, if even there.

Or, on the other hand, we go through the equal abomination of so-called automatic promotion. Promotion to what? From one meaningless classification to another. I see absolutely no point

to a graded curriculum at all, neither educationally nor administra-
tively, assuming one can make such a distinction between these
needs in the educational process. A graded curriculum is not only
pointless, but it generates terrible and unnecessary difficulties in
the administration of education, not to mention the even greater
difficulties it creates for good teaching. More than that; it guarantees that we will not be able to do anything effective about providing equal education for unequal children. And we shall certainly never make any dent at all on existing inequities if we persist
with our graded curricula.

Set all the goals you want; inspire aspirations; create hopes
and desires. But make sure these are attuned to children, their
individual qualities and abilities, their learning situations of the
moment, and not to the agricultural cycle of harvesting and plant-
ing, nor to some meaningless notion that schooling should last six
or eight or twelve years.

(2) The second fundamental requirement from the makers of
school policy and the providers of school resources is something
so starkly simple and yet so fundamental that it is one of the
elusive mysteries of the world how it manages to be ignored, or
perverted, or distorted so readily and so frequently. It is this: That
if a teacher is to have any chance at all sensitively to perceive,
understand and relate effectively to the children in front of her,
and hence to teach them by her and their own lights, she simply
must have time and energy to do so, assuming she has the training requisite to it as well. There is no way to achieve this simple
and indispensable goal except through individuation of education,
and that simply means time, energy, and interest. To assume that
sensitive, individuated education can transpire in classrooms of
thirty children, which the teacher confronts five hours a day or
more, is ridiculous beyond comment. I know that in making these
remarks I shall immediately be said to be a wild-eyed dreamer
without any sense for the realities of the situation. But let's see
what the realities are.

There are two basic meanings of practical, or realistic: One
of them is treacherous, or can be; the other is genuine and fundamental. Most ordinarily we say something is practical or realistic
if we think it can be achieved within the limits of existing values
and attitudes. The realistic in this sense is what is politically pos-

sible. But what is politically possible may have nothing to do at all with what is absolutely indispensable to one's goals. It is, for instance, politically realistic and hence practical to get money to build bigger and more jails and reformatories. And so long as we focus on these policies, these eminently practical policies, we shall continue to fill the jails and the reformatories before they are even built. The same goes for the usual policies regarding mental illness, for alcoholism, for drug addiction, and marital unhappiness. The practical things—namely the politically feasible things—not only don't do anything about solving problems to which they are directed, they guarantee the continuation and the intensification of those problems. The analogy to sickness and its symptoms is too apt not to insist upon it. Perhaps an equally good analogy is to shaving. Every morning I shave the hairs off my face. Every morning they start to grow back, even as I am shaving, and sure enough every next morning there I am with hairs on my face that need to be shaved. Prisons, reformatories, and our politically practical and feasible school policies do as much to eliminate the problems to which they are directed as shaving contributes to the elimination of hairs on my face. Classrooms of thirty or more children, taught five or more hours a day, may be all that it is politically possible to achieve. But if that's all, then that's what we will continue to get —mass meaningless education—or at least something very, very different from individuated education. And certainly something worlds apart from any decent version of equal education for unequal children.

Applying these notions of practicality and feasibility to our education problems, one must insist that many of the policies which may be impractical in the limited sense of politically possible are eminently practical in the sense that without them nothing much good can be hoped for. I suppose one can put it somewhat less starkly by saying that any genuine movement toward our desired goals—individuated education and equal education—demands far more out of policy makers and the public than is now deemed politically possible. I am not sure that every little bit helps, nor that half a loaf is better than none. It may be. But we shall have to take each issue in turn and ask whether the proposed compromises with what we know ought to be done really make enough of a difference to be worth the effort they require to get them done and the obvious detraction of time, energy, and focus from the real problems and solutions.

What we obviously need are far many more teachers, far many more schools, much more money for all the appurtenances of educational procedures. There is no way to move effectively toward individuated education and hence toward equal education without revolutionary increases in resources.

One is tempted by these considerations to say that any city gets about the kind of educational system it deserves. But obviously this is a spurious doctrine, since not everyone has an equal voice in determining what kind of educational system we shall have, and so many of our people and their children get much better education than they deserve, judging by their do-nothing attitudes and their congenital reluctance to pay for what they demand.

The facts about quality of teachers are well known, for instance. We won't get revolutionary upsurges in the quality of teachers and teacher training simply by increasing the financial returns and rewards. But we surely won't even get a worm's tail of a difference if we don't put a lot more money into teacher's salaries. We may not like the idea of having to try to attract good people to teaching and getting them well trained by the bait of monetary rewards. But this is a monetarily competitive and monetarily judging culture. And no one has a right to expect teachers to have different motivational systems than those that characterize business men, doctors, lawyers, and all the so-called leaders of our society. No one has a right to expect more dedication and selflessness and indifference to material rewards from teachers than from anyone else. And yet it is astounding how much dedication and selflessness we do get out of teachers, perfectly astounding. I continue to marvel that anyone stays in the profession at all. We must all be some sort of queer people. And as for any parent who thinks teachers are overpaid—even the obvious dodos in the profession—I venture to say that one or perhaps at most two days serving as a teacher in the average urban classroom, plus all the ancillary preparations and extracurricular duties, will convince even the most obdurate critic that to be a teacher is not exactly to lead the good life.

All these matters have been rehashed and re-rehashed so often it seems a pity to waste any time saying them, especially to this audience. But perhaps they bear repetition simply because, being so obvious, they tend to get overlooked from time to time, or, worse still, they are ignored on the grounds that they represent crass materialism. And if we are concerned with motivational systems, we had better quickly understand that if social disesteem and degradation, and inadequate rewards for responsibilities produce the problems in our underprivileged children, they do exactly the same to our adult populations as well. The fact of the matter seems to be that this far we are lucky—luckier than we deserve—for, instead of getting just what we are paying for, we are on the average getting something far more and far better than what we are paying for—at least as far as teacher performance is concerned.

(3) The third and, for now, last policy requirement I would mention, as necessary support for the teachers as they try to provide individuated and equal deductions, is really twofold: There is, on the one hand, the absolute necessity that teachers shall feel supported all the way down the line in their efforts by their supervisory personnel at all reaches of school administration. Principals and supervisors who toss problems back to teachers and try to force them to solve problems arising from the behavior of various kinds of disturbed children in the classroom are only injuring everyone concerned—all the children plus the teacher plus the whole school system. But that is only one aspect of support. More important is this consideration: equal and equally good individuated education demands that the schools should cease immediately and forever from being conducted as talent-scout agencies. We are not, as educators, in the business of seeking out rare and commercially valuable talents. We are not running art galleries or troupes of performing horses. We are in the business of educating all children, whatever their talents, whatever their abilities. It is their right and our obligation. We are a farce rather than a democratic school system if we build our schools and their structures of internal rewards around the notion of special places for those children who by virtue of lucky birth and or lucky upbringing can perform more adequately the tasks we have set them. To reward some is to punish others. No one has ever yet demonstrated that anyone who performs poorly in a competitive situation is improved either in his motivations or his capacities by being publicly slighted, even implicitly. There is simply no good evidence about what happens to the motivational structure of lower-performing

children when their lower levels of performance are negatively symbolized with public rituals every quarter or every exhibit or every auditorium. This is an antiquated theory of motivation, generated by and serving the very special interests in an elite.

To reward some children for so-called high levels of performance and implicitly degrade or punish others for lower levels is in fact to reinstate an ancient aristocratic notion that the well-born deserve what they have because they are well born. What more can we conceivably ask of a child than that he shall give us all that of which he is psychologically and mentally able to give at any moment? And if he gives us his best available, on what conceivable grounds can we then degrade him and fail to give him as much as we give any and all other students simply because his level of achievement is not equal to theirs? Differences in performance are the result of either differences in hereditary endowment or environmental opportunities or both. Shall we, then, continue to reward differences in hereditary endowment and environmental opportunities? On what conceivable grounds could that be made consonant with democratic theory and practice?

I sometimes feel it is hopeless to keep saying these things because, no matter how often they are said and assented to, superintendents keep vying with each other in terms of outstanding performances of students, and hence pressure the principals to vie with each other on the same grounds, and they in turn pressure the teachers, and they in turn pressure the students. We are out after excellence—indeed, whatever excellence each child has in him. And each child's own particular excellence, however mediocre it may be judged by artificial comparative standards, is and must be as equally valuable to us in the classroom as that of any other child. That much is indispensable to equal and equally good education. Without such a perspective we go nowhere. Let us stop measuring schools in terms of the number of merit scholars, or winners of national competitions, or exhibits sent to galleries. We are glad for these contributions to our culture. But that is not what schools are for.

Finally, I turn to the third phase of equal education. We have looked at the first two phases, the first referring to the pre-school experiences and general social situation of the child; the second deals with the in-school experiences that what is needed from teachers and principals here. The third phase refers to the post-school horizons and prospects of the students. Again with this audience I need not go into the details of why and how one's future aspirations and hopes importantly shape one's behavior in the present. And yet we seem to forget this when we deal with underprivileged children who don't have much, or as much, to look forward to as our better-off children. We can't hope that school, and high motivation, and punctuality, and cleanliness, and all the little teachers' goodies will be as important to them as they will be to children who are college bound, and more. We can hope and pray that some of the less-privileged children will be touched off and inspired to struggle nevertheless. Again it is astounding how many kids do entertain high hopes against the realistic predictions and probabilities to the contrary. But so long as the probable and predictable futures involve tasks and ways of life to which school and school achievement seem only dimly if at all relevant, we cannot realistically hope for high morale, motivation, and integration into the idea and practice of education.

The outside social environment representing the future of the child is thus terribly important as a factor affecting his capacities and his performances in school. Again, then, social engineering, designed to alter the system of distribution of adult opportunities and rewards, is a fundamental requirement for any effective movement toward equal education during the school years. And here is where the teacher and all people connected with the school have a special obligation to the underprivileged child, namely, to try to relate to him and work with him in such a way as to help him risk himself against the probabilities, to help him cast a longing eye upon what might be his for the effort, the special effort he must make, as against what is surely going to be his lot if he makes only the predictable effort. In that way we might make some small difference in helping to make education a little more equal for such children than it will otherwise surely be.

I have deliberately refrained, it must be evident, from dealing with concrete problems of techniques and procedures, involving such questions as whether to bus children out of their districts or not, whether to have special classes or not, whether to have ability groupings or not, whether to increase or remove programs of higher horizons. These are matters which are to be settled either by fiat and bias, without research evidence, or to be taken on gingerly and tenatively, without bias, and subject to continuing evaluation so that we shall know better than we now know whether they do any good at all. At best these are all obvious and sometimes shabby compromises with the real article. Homogeneous ability groupings are shabby compromises with individuated education and in any event do not avoid the problems of heterogenity. Bussing kids out of their neighborhood is a shabby, though perhaps unavoidable, compromise with genuine desegregation of neighborhoods and schools. Higher horizons may only be like applying Band Aids to a cancerous sore. We do not really know. And since we do not really know, we cannot scream loudly for or against. Probably the maximum value gained from some of these compromises is some small advantage for some limited number of children at the cost of others; sometimes the major value gained is that pride is maintained, and probably it ought to be if nothing else can be gotten out of the situation. But there are any number of documents arguing the pros and cons of these techniques and methods and I do not wish to go into them, however much I may recognize they represent the day-to-day realities of the problems faced by school administrators, teachers, parents, and pupils.

I think it more important that we shall here consider the minimum conditions required for equal and equally good education for all children. For that is what integration finally means. If integration is to have any significance at all, it can only mean a condition under which all children, regardless of color, religion, and ability, get from us and our country equal and equally good educations. That the problem at the moment focuses on the Negro-White split is historically temporary. Not temporary—but permanently with us—is the problem of equal education over the whole range of variabilities that our population will present forever, as long as we remain in the human species. To that end, toward the working solution of that problem of variability, we must direct our attention to the pre-school factors, the social environments, the in-school variables, and the postschool probabilities and horizons, as these all come severely and critically to influence the capacity of our children to secure equal benefit from the educational facilities we provide. Our schools determine our future, not just our educational future, but our whole future as a people and as a nation. We cannot therefore even for a moment fail to engage in the basic problems of social engineering of the entire fabric of our society that in different ways and degrees impinges upon the conduct of our schools.

I remind you, and myself, all of us, that in a very basic way, as we go in this educational experiment, so, perhaps, goes the entire world. We cannot afford to fail.

Considering the difficulties we face, we have done extraordinarily well so far, all low-brow critics to the contrary. Relative to any other major nation, ours is indisputably the most successful school system, by far, by any major and important criterion. But relative to what we could be, to what we must be and become, if we are to realize our democratic ideals, and to provide equal opportunity to all our citizens, we have miles and miles to go. Let us start.

Dimensions of the School's Role in the Problems of Integration

Martin Deutsch
Director, Institute for Developmental Studies
Associate Professor, Department of Psychiatry
New York Medical College

There is so very much that has been said at this conference that by now it is fairly easy to overlap with some of the previous speakers. But there are some points that I would like to make this morning. Some of them have been made, but I think in a somewhat different context from that in which I would like to present them here today.

We often move from the social level to the psychological level to the educational with a great ease, maybe with too much ease. Often we lose thereby a real appreciation of what some of the transitional determinants might be. Particularly is this so when we are concerned with the education of all children and with the kinds of major changes in social structure that are required by the Supreme Court decisions and by the changes in American life in the last decade. We now ask, what can a school system accomplish? I think this is what we have been asking in this conference. What can we accomplish to make integration meaningful and what are some of the antecedents required in order to produce a social basis for work toward a truly integrated experience for the child?

I think we have to recognize that in one sense the future is in the present and that it is the school's role to channelize the present toward the future. Now, this carries with it certain very special responsibilities. The school has become a pivotal point of a very real social struggle: the struggle for the full realization of our social potential, the struggle for the kinds of social equality that will result in the maximizing of opportunities for all children. It

is also—and I feel it is only—through education that disproportionate subgroup concentration in the lower socio-economic groups
can be influenced so that at least social-class barriers to true
integration will be minimized. Many of the barriers we have been
talking about at this conference are social-class barriers, but they
have become caste as well as class barriers because of the particular history surrounding the institution of slavery and the period
after the Emancipation Proclamation.

There is no longer any question of the critical role of the environment in the growth of the child. The major questions that
remain here relate to the specifics of the interaction between environment and development and the differentials which may exist
in the potency of various influences at different stages of development. Segregation is an aspect of experience in the growing-up of
both Negro and white children, and this experience plays a crucial
role in determining their developing attitudes toward the self and
toward the human condition. It must be obvious, further, that an
essentially nondemocratic experience does not foster the growth
of a democratic value system.

Now, it should be recognized that, with the kinds of inadequate
environment that were described yesterday, and that have been
described at many places, and that I also have talked about in
other papers, many children will not be offered an opportunity to reach their full potential. As long as institutionalized
forms of discrimination are maintained, as long as Negro and white
children do not have a chance to touch the future in the present
through integrated experiences that are meaningful, neither group
is being adequately prepared for the future. I think this is a vital
point because it is now clear to all but the Neanderthals that the
future will see an integrated America. Social change, though we
might not see it from our particular point, is moving quite rapidly,
and the momentum is likely to increase considerably as time goes
on. Certainly what is now termed the social revolution of 1963 has
underlined this.

Segregated conditions play a particularly invidious role in the
child's growing up. They create an incorrect picture of America
and an incorrect picture of what kinds and types and forms of
human relations are possible. But, in a more specific psychological sense, they do not give the Negro, Puerto Rican, or most

other minority group children the tools for handling daily inter-group, interpersonal relationships or the strategies that are instrumental for handling the kinds of problems that must be overcome to achieve individual success in our society. An example of this would be the role vicissitudes involved in locating and negotiating for a job.

If the school is to play a major role in at least partially compensating for the unhealthy kinds of environments associated with poverty and segregation, one has first to assume that this is a desirable role for it. My assumption is that this is in fact a necessary role; I can identify no other institution that is in the position of the school to influence significantly the development of all children.

We at this conference share this conviction that the school must be a vital institution in the whole process of social change. The struggles around questions of strategies and goals of integration could lead to a real revitalization of education. The problems surrounding the integration question go to the core of the guiding philosophies in American education and place the educator in the role of an engineer of social change. There are many other social forces that we would like to see play a role, but one cannot sit back and wait and hope that social change will take place simultaneously on every level. One has to identify the influential elements that can be introduced from one's own daily activities; for us here this means dealing with the problem of the child and the school.

As the school gets oriented toward this role—sometimes on its own volition, sometimes with much external pushing and shoving—certain limitations emerge which are inherent in its own structure, history, and organization, and in the social context in which it finds itself.

To digress for a moment: It is interesting to note a particular confluence of events. At the time of the first Sputnik, great anxiety was expressed as to inadequacies in the American educational system. Many suggestions were made for major alterations and most especially for more status and prestige for the educational system and its personnel in a general recognition of their role in the over-all development of the child's intellectual, creative, and general psychological capabilities. Aside, however, from some content changes in curricula and a generally healthy focusing on problems of intellectual development, relatively little change accrued from discussion of this so-called "crisis." However, the then-recognized need for major institutional modifications emerges most dramatically in the present very real crisis surrounding, generally, the integration problem and, specifically, the issue of facilitating the development of the individual potential in America's underprivileged. This not only alters the consciousness of educators in regard to a section of the population, but of necessity improves the possibilities for real basic alterations in both structure and philosophy that will have positive influence on the development of all youth, i.e., privileged and underprivileged. In this sense, the struggle for an integrated America offers an opportunity for a most critical evaluation of present inadequacies in the educational system and accomplishes what the external competitive condition—i.e., Sputnik—could not.

Let us return, though, to a consideration of the obstacles in the way of the school's assumption of major new roles.

Some of the limitations come from the larger social community. The ambivalence of much of the community to allow complete integration must be recognized; for example, there are advantages for the status quo in having a large, low-paid, marginal population. Such economic factors and the attendant psychological conditions of a pecking hierarchy yield to some the facade of automatic status and superiority, and here we find a source of some of the ambivalence and much of the hostility toward integration.

I would hypothesize that the corruption of human potential that is inherent in all situations where there exist caste and class symbols for superior and inferior status is virulent in a classroom which reflects these conditions. Too often, rewards are based not on individual accomplishment, but on things like tested intelligence levels, race, and father's occupation. A major obstacle, then, which must be overcome is the intrusion of these values into the classroom. To do so, preservice and in-service training must assist the teacher to perceive social relationships from a broader perspective than her own class position. In a sense, not to prepare the teacher to be able to do this could effectively sabotage meaningful integration.

Another obstacle is the historical drag of the actual behavior systems which are at variance with the explicit value system. This makes it difficult for teachers and administrators—who are often under pressure—to recognize that much must be altered in terms of the new matrix of our social system, in terms of the demand for equality and in terms of what equality really means. This carries with it the conviction that social contradiction can, to some extent, be handled through the processes of the school. To accomplish this objective, the school, with reference to other institutions, should demand an unequally large amount of funds, educationally qualified individuals, institutional structures, experimental programs, and what have you, in order to create maximally fostering conditions for the realization of individual potential for the child from a deprived environment. This is, I think, one of the basic principles with which we have to concern ourselves. *If society takes away, if society has maintained a hundred years of second-class citizenship for the Negro, if society always insists that new migrants—regardless of what ethnic group—maintain some kind of secondary citizenship for a few generations, then it becomes society's role to compensate for this loss*—and it is a tremendous loss of potential. This is especially true now as so many of the traditional steps on the occupational ladder are disappearing with increasing technology. More and more America is confronted with a large mass of unskilled, unemployed people, a disproportionately high percentage of whom come from minority groups, while there are many skilled, relatively highly specialized and paid, occupational categories searching for workers.

As was previously pointed out, the school has an important role in society's compensation for the situation. But there will always be some lag, some segment where the child has not caught up, as long as we have a society that allows discriminatory conditions and, most important, is not actively engaged in giving behavioral reality to its explicit democratic value system. That means an active, intense, frontal struggle for meaningful integration. Further, if the schools are to be successful in their efforts, the first demand must be for the support and enrichment of the school system itself by the community.

Related to problems of compensation is another obstacle; it arises from the failure to plan for social change, so that occupational and economic necessities change faster than either static institutional situations or human beings can accommodate to. This is again a rather crucial element in the school situation. So much development and modification have taken place, and there has been such very real change in urban America, that the school has had created for it much more than its previous passive educational role. It can no longer simply receive children and test, grade, and categorize them without reference to their individual social backgrounds, their latent and manifest cognitive strengths, their attitudes toward learning, and their aspirations. Instead, it is becoming a very active participant in preventing certain forms of mental illness and in preventing juvenile delinquency, and on a more positive side, in really developing human potential to the maximum level of which the individual is capable.

Now, if we do not become discouraged by more social microscopic conditions that inhibit change, and we, instead, look especially at the school and what the possibilities might be there, the school—as the most sensitive, and as one of the most significant points for social change—has a problem in itself. It has, so often, and certainly in all large urban areas, become a bureaucratic dinosaur, and now is being asked to funnel, digest, and utilize the work of the human sciences and of education in a creative manner to handle social problems. This involves a degree of social engineering that I don't think is asked of any other institution. The magnitude of the task does not mean that one has to be patient while these obstacles are worked with, but it does mean that the system has to plan, to have conferences like this, to re-think the fundamental issues, and to come out of it with some kinds of systematic formats for operations and changes in the educational structure and in educational curricula.

There are a few points here that relate to what the school can do on an everyday basis in order to accomplish some of the objectives discussed here. One is in terms of the educational apparatus itself, another is in terms of the enrichment of the child, and a third relates to the larger community.

Let us consider first an aspect of the educational apparatus.

In response to challenge, education has the disadvantage of a long and encumbering history. In a sense, the institution of education—the school—is the *status quo*. It often operates through huge politically oriented bureaucracies that continually inhibit its potential for change and for developing strategies for meeting social crises such as those inherent in the new urban America. These bureaucracies are often so large that introduction of meaningful change, even when agreed on by the higher echelons, is limited by the clogging of communication channels with paper, red tape, and assorted other artifacts, and by the constraints under which the average classroom teacher operates. A chasm is created between policy and implementation, and as a result many inconsistencies are produced. For example, well thought-out and efficient systems are instituted for bussing children across districts to accomplish physical integration, but too often once the children are in the new school a laissez-faire attitude prevails. There are too many children who sit in a segregated island in a so-called integrated classroom, with there being no real attempt to help the children establish some intergroup, interpersonal knowledge and relationship. One way of doing this, for example, in a newly integrated classroom would be to use a simple autobiographical method, where each child tells something about himself and his interests and aspirations, so that through the formal structure of the classroom children will have a basis for accumulating a little personal knowledge of each other as individuals.

While, of course, the school cannot assure that children in the same classroom will relate to each other well, particularly when there are large social class differences, it can be aware of the problem and devise techniques, such as the one suggested above, within the formal curriculum, to increase the probability of interpersonal relationships. Here is where it is necessary for specialists in disciplines such as anthropology, sociology, and social psychology to be actively involved in evaluating and guiding this process. They can not only help to devise specific methods and techniques, but they can give in-service training to teachers and administrators aimed at helping them to understand the problems of socio-cultural dissonance. The social science specialists should have considerable independence, so that they do not become cannibalized and digested by the bureaucracy; at the same time they should function as an indigenous part of the school system.

The suggestion of social science contributions to school integration within the context of discussing the activities of the school system with regard to its own organization stems from the understanding that physical integration can be considered only a first step in the process. Physical integration is a necessary step, but it must not be confused with the goal of compensating the child for experiential deprivation which interferes with his receptivity to the learning process, and prevents him from participating and competing on the basis of his own abilities. Successful participation involves a whole complex of social and psychological factors, including self-image, achievement motivation, sensory and linguistic development, and the like. The effects of discrimination and impoverishment on these attributes have been discussed extensively in the recent literature. However, in the context of the school's role in integration, the nullification of these detrimental consequences is the major goal. It is here that the active participation of school personnel is so necessary, and it is here that education has the opportunity both structurally and functionally to reorient itself to changing social realities.

Simple mechanical implementation of physical integration can make a farce of real integration. I have seen too many administrators and teachers who see integration as an unwelcome threat to the *status quo* and their "power prerogatives," and these people can nullify real implementation. It is necessary for the system to have the flexibility to reeducate or remove such personnel. It must be stated that many of the people who thus impede real progress do so through a dedication to the bureaucratic forms in which education has so often immobilized itself, rather than through any active desire to frustrate the goals, though in many instances this may be accompanied by highly internalized social class prejudices based on a different orientation toward life and differing expectations of children's behavior and performance. For example, I have noted in in-service courses the tendency on the part of some teachers to engage in extremely tenuous psychologizing of the children's behavior and reactions. Particularly does this occur around the interpretation of hyperactivity, attentional shifting, and inhibited communication with the teacher. Actually, non-middle-class children do not, for the most part, conform to middle-class classroom behavior mores, and the teacher interprets the apparent withdrawal of the child in psychological—or pseudo-psychological —terms. It is true that the teacher does not receive from these children the kinds of reinforcement that come from an actively expressed curiosity and from an uninhibited verbal rapport. This places on the teacher an extra responsibility to delay her gratification until she has won the trust of the children and successfully interpreted to them the demands of the school situation. Standard teacher training as yet does not equip the teacher with the understanding and techniques necessary to accomplish this. So it becomes the responsibility of the school itself—and particularly the urban school—to provide the appropriate in-service training to both new and experienced teachers and administrators. In the absence of such training, it is hard to know how effective school personnel can be in fostering the true goals of integration.

A much-discussed major issue in the organization of integrated schools is that of heterogeneous versus homogeneous ability groupings. Within the normal intellectual range there may be strong arguments for homogeneous grouping, but at the same time there are also sound arguments for the heterogeneous organization. When we consider the classroom which contains children of widely differing backgrounds, the issue becomes more than simply one for educational argument. In a general sense, this problem is becoming more important with bussing of children, redefining of neighborhood boundaries, and, most important, because it will probably most influence the composition of school populations, the locating of many new schools in border areas. These actions have the effect of insuring heterogeneity of background of children in each classroom. Under these conditions, homogeneous grouping creates *de facto* segregation in the classroom. Therefore, if there are to be integrated experiences there must be heterogeneous groupings.

Though this is not the place to go into it, there are also strong arguments as to possible advantages in the homogeneous learning situation. However, with the overlap between deprived circumstances and minority group membership, there will be a bunching up of minority group scores at the lower end of the continuum. Homogeneous grouping serves to underline the racial category with a derivative of it, which is secondary status in the classroom. It is true that this is often disguised by assigning noninvidious identifications to the ability groupings, but I have yet to meet a child who cannot identify his ascribed status. If heterogeneous grouping makes for some unfairness to the majority group child, that is simply the price that must now be paid for 100 years of segregation and lack of attention to the special educational problems of the minority child. The better and the faster the school can adjust to and formulate curricula consistent with our changed urban society, the lower the price will be. In other words, the school should not extract a further price from the minority group child for integration, but instead tax itself to develop techniques that are appropriate for groups of diversified ability. This is essentially now a moral issue, and the learning situation has enough inherent strength to encompass the forms that will be demanded. Basically, the track system is an example of the unwillingness of the community to pay the price. Its use can easily become extremely rigidified, and despite efforts to the contrary, it locks many children within early-determined expectation and accomplishment boundaries.

Another problem of homogeneous groupings, and most specifically of an all-pervasive track system, is the determination of the teacher's expectations of the child and her inevitable, even if unintentional, communication of these to the child. As so often happens in the development of any system, the doors of each compartment become locked, and what is created is an intellectual ghetto. The fact that some administrators point to cracks in the wall—and a few children do squeeze through these cracks—does not reduce the reality of the closed doors. It is objectively very difficult to get away from differing sets of expectations for the children in different tracks or groups. These expectations seep into the teacher-child interaction and into the learning process. A tendency develops to reduce the level of the stimuli presented to conform with the expectations of the child's performance. When a particular child answers a question correctly, instead of consciously raising the demand level for him, the tendency is to keep this level constant for a period of time and thus adjust to the performance expectations for the group. So what is developed is a kind of compression system. While the argument is often advanced that heterogeneous groupings can be unfair to the child who is farthest from the group norm, the same can be said of the homogeneous group, especially as regards the child who is intellectually starting to move and reaching in the direction of his potential.

Another overriding consideration that relates to the total school experience and to all aspects of integration is the development of the child's self-image and the need to help him to build a sense of respect for himself and his intellectual capabilities, whatever they may be. The lower-class child experiences the middle-class oriented school as discontinuous with his home environment and comes relatively poorly prepared in the basic skills on which the curriculum is founded. The school becomes a place which makes puzzling demands and where failure is frequent and feelings of competence are subsequently not generated. The best theoretical model for thinking about this, I think, is White's theory of competence motivation.* He points out that experiences of success and accomplishment engender feelings of competence which in turn generate primary motivation. As was indicated, the school experiences of the socially deprived child do not easily yield success, and special effort and programming are required to build motivation.

So often the school experience is an intellectually frustrating one as the child is always being compared and graded, if not any longer on a racial basis, on an intellectual and personality one. He is being compared with his teacher's model-image of middle-class children, with his classmates, with national norms, with the highest achieving youngster in his class, etc. We could have a much more motivating and a much more democratic educational system if each child were instead, in effect, used as his own control by having each successive performance compared with the previous performance. In this way, a child's performance could be evaluated not on the cross-sectional aspects of achievement, but on the longitudinal axis. The child's failures would be in terms of his own antecedent scores rather than competitively determined by the performance of others. He would be able to achieve real gratification from accomplishments that compare favorably to other children in terms of magnitude of improvement rather than placement on the achievement hierarchy. This would be one way of nullifying the accumulated frustrations so often for

* White, R. "Motivation Reconsidered: The Concept of Competence," *Psychological Review,* LXVI (1959), 297-333.

these children associated with intellectual activities, and particularly with early school experience. When we talk about the school compensating a child for life inequalities, much of that compensation must be in the area of building motivation and finding ways of creating more positive concepts in regard to both the self and the intellective activities.

It is again in this area that the mechanical application of integration could have additional harmful implications. In order to get away from prejudice, many school systems have dropped all reference to really crucial life variables like race. In essence, I think this represents a most invidious form of prejudice. Children cannot grow up with a consistent and positive concept of the self if the fact of being Indian or Negro becomes a source of embarrassment or something that for some reason the environment insists on not mentioning. The fact of being Negro or white can no more be ignored than can that of being boy or girl, as it carries with it certain on-going personal, social, and cultural connotations. Teachers, both white and Negro, must be helped to deal with questions of race and intergroup relations on an objective, frank, professional basis, or their embarrassment and circumventing of the issue will somehow always be communicated to the child, and to the Negro child the connotation attached will be a negative one and will have a depressing influence on his motivation and social integration in mixed groups.

This discussion has consistently returned to the vital role of the adult, most particularly the teacher, in influencing the child's developing self and social perceptions through her interaction with him. Another aspect of the child's performance around which this process takes place is intelligence test scores. I do not here want to go into the question of the validity of the IQ, beyond observing that with increasing massive social intervention it should increasingly become a much poorer predictor of school success for the child from marginal circumstances. Rather, I want to point out that the child's IQ score—no matter how valid or invalid as a predictor of later achievement—can become the basis for the teacher's expectations of his performance, and through a variant of the process delineated earlier, can come to have a large and negative influence on his school progress. Again, in terms of the whole question of self-image and building a psychology of competence, it might be worthwhile to use the intelligence test only as a clinical diagnostic instrument. In this way, another potential source of negative feedback could be eliminated.

If, though, the schools insist on the maintenance of the IQ, there is potentially a way of working it out, though much investigation is still required. In a symposium at the American Psychological Association meetings in 1960, Otto Klineberg pointed out that one can anticipate that children from underprivileged areas will have lower IQ's along certain dimensions, and that these dimensions can potentially be identified and perhaps some formula can be constructed to allow for the effects of background inequities. At the recent meetings of the Society for Research in Child Development, I reported some data we have collected at the Institute for Developmental Studies which demonstrate that, when controlling for social class, fifth-grade Negro children without fathers in the home tested significantly lower than similar children with fathers in the home. Concomitantly, Negro lower-class children with preschool experience tested significantly higher than those without such experience. What the intervening variables might be is not relevant here, though one could speculate that they might have something to do with the presence or absence of opportunities for increased adult-child interaction. The point is that there are environmental circumstances that play a direct role in lowering IQ's and that the result of these circumstances should not be codified in the school records and form a basis for the child's curriculum or for the teacher's interpretations. Hopefully, we will some day come to the point where we can have a whole series of multiple equations by which one can recognize that a certain set of circumstances will yield a particular set of consequences. For example, the absence of a preschool experience would perhaps be worth three or four IQ points; certain specific levels of poverty and deprivation, the existence of discrimination or experience of certain types of discrimination, the existence or the nonexistence of a father in the home, and the like, could also be judged as to their value in IQ points, and a score could be calculated for each child on the basis of such formulas.

No matter what the circumstances, children cannot be helped to develop their potential intellectual strengths if the community and society do not supply the school system with the funds to create the therapeutic tools to do the job. One of the keys to successful integration is the facilitation of intellectual and psychological growth so that the detrimental influences associated with poverty can be overcome by the focused efforts of reoriented school curricula. Of course, there are other interrelated roads: housing, jobs—the whole social macrocosm. But our job here is to concentrate on that area in which we hopefully have some small influence.

In other places I have emphasized the importance of utilizing behavioral science knowledge in programming learning sequences, in training teachers in the social aspects of the learning process, and, most particularly, in the development of specialized, systematic enrichment programs, with low teacher-pupil ratios, fulltime kindergartens, intensive preschool experiences, and ungraded early grade sequences. If society will not supply the money for these things, the schools will fail to accomplish what the current social situation requires. In this rich, abundant economy of ours, the funds must be there. And when human need and our need as a society for the potential contributions from all people are strongly enough recognized, the funds will be made available, especially when social survival may be dependent on the development of these human resources. But even with the funds, the schools could fail if they are not ready for the metamorphosis to the active role previously discussed. Programs to reverse the effects of deprivation cannot be put together in a day, and people can't be trained in a month to carry them through. This has been a consistent weakness of many programs which have been established. The children, society, and the problem deserve teachers and administrators who have been extensively trained and selected to do the job. Also, programs to raise the horizons of children must not be allowed to be dominated by public relations needs, or by an urgent requirement to get results. It is necessary for programs to be rigorously evaluated, carefully researched, to be conducted on an interdisciplinary basis—for all the human sciences have a lot to contribute—and it must be recognized that it is better to get results a year later and for these results to have depth and a temporal stability, than for ephemeral changes to be registered quickly.

A note of caution as to the choice of methods best to insure the goals of integration. We must be concerned that even with open enrollment and bussing, the location of neighborhood schools be consciously planned wherever possible in such a way as to draw on a heterogeneous population. The point here is that open enrollment, bussing, etc., places an extra burden on the minority group child and his parents, and wherever this can be eliminated through re-zoning, new construction, and the like, it should be done, thereby not placing the burden of change on the child.

There may be certain circumstances where the physical conditions of integration may be of less immediate importance than establishing the most fostering environment for cognitive growth. For example, where one or two hours daily spent in the whole bussing operation is necessary, it might be too much to require of a child in order just to sit with white children in some distant neighborhood. It might be better if we keep in mind the eventual aims and goals, and have the child spend three hours in a type of all-day neighborhood school, fully equipped to offer the most fostering and most highly developed educational experience for him. I would also be somewhat concerned about bussing middle-class white or Negro children into slum areas. It is not that this would necessarily be bad for the children, but that it could do great damage to the potential for integrating schools by provoking irrational fears on the part of parents, resulting in the massive withdrawal of middle-class children—both white and Negro—from the public schools, and creating a completely class and caste segregated public school system. The danger here is particularly apparent in regard to people of newly arrived middle-class status, as one of the major sources of intergroup conflict is the perceived threat to newly achieved but insecurely held social status. This does not mean that the insistence on middle-class or lower-class children having to travel to boundary areas should relax, nor does it mean that children should not be bussed from one district to another. Rather, what I am saying is that bussing, for example, which at best is one of many possible steps in the right direction, should not be confused with the goals of eventual indigenous integration. Neither should its use be seen as an end in itself and permit the schools to relax after they have worked out bussing arrangements. There is always the danger that a bureaucratic system will for all practical purposes rest content with the form and mechanics of integration. As previously pointed out, what goes on in the classroom is the real issue. It is only through a massive improvement of his educational experience that the child will develop the abilities to achieve more secure social status. Thereby a basis will also be established for full social integration.

It can be noted that the bulk of this discussion relates to counteracting the effects of poverty, segregation, and attendant deprivation and reflects areas needing special attention if the integrated experience is to be interpreted meaningfully by the school for the child. Of course, in the broadest sense, the objective is to assist children in the realization of individual potential leading to the jumping of social class boundaries. The eventual aim of school integration, thought of in this social context, is to eliminate the largely ethnic basis of social class membership and to create conditions in which basic ability will be the determinant of social mobility, and of individual self-realization.

School Integration: A Puerto Rican View

Joseph Monserrat
Director, Migration Division, Department of Labor
Commonwealth of Puerto Rico

I welcome this opportunity to discuss with you what has been called a "Puerto Rican View of School Integration." This title would seem to imply that Puerto Ricans have their own view on the question of school integration, somewhat differently from others. As a matter of fact—we do!

To understand *how* we Puerto Ricans see this issue of integration and *why* we see it as we do—what integration means and does not mean to us—requires an understanding of our experiences and conditioning as well as our view of the total issue. It is equally necessary and important to bear in mind clearly the experiences and conditioning of the American Negro if we are to fully understand all the issues inherent in the struggle for integration in New York City and the rest of the nation.

The present struggle for desegregation and for integration in schools is not just a struggle to secure truly equal educational opportunities for members of the Negro community of America. At *this* particular moment in the history and dynamics of this struggle, the pertinent sentence of the Supreme Court decision is *not* the one that reads, "Segregation with the sanction of the law has a tendency to retard the educational and mental development of Negro children and to deprive them of some benefits they would receive in a racially integrated school system." The really pertinent and significant statement of the May 17 decision *now,* at *this* moment, is the one that reads, "To separate them [Negroes] from others of similar age and qualifications solely because of their race generates a feeling of inferiority as to their status in the community that may affect their hearts and minds in a way unlikely ever to be undone."

The judicial tempering of this statement by saying *"may affect"* could have been left out. The fact of history clearly demonstrates

45

that this type of segregation, along with all other types of segregation, *has* in fact affected the "hearts and minds" of our American Negro community in a way that most certainly would "unlikely ever be undone" if it were not for the affirmative action being taken by the Negro in America today, a century after the signing of the Emancipation Proclamation.

Segregation, as practiced in our society against the Negro, can be understood only as a part of his tragic history in America; it can be understood in terms of how he came to the United States and how he was been dealt with by the majority society since his arrival.

The stigma of inferiority became a means of enforcing a negative self-evaluation upon the victim. It also provides the justification for the oppressiveness of the oppressors, and while this stigma has been and still is used against others in America, its greatest effect has been against the Negro.

Unlike the Puerto Rican of today, or the Irish, the German, or the Jew of yesterday, the Negro did not come here as a free man seeking to better his opportunities in a new environment. His relationship with his homeland, its history and civilization, its language and forms of worship was forcibly broken. He was not just disarmed physically—he was disarmed psychologically.

That tremendous and untold damage has also been done to the majority group—including not only the old-line Americans, but the millions of others who followed and who, though citizens of the United States today, were born in other countries yesterday or are children of those who were—is also implicit in the Supreme Court opinion. It can be said—more, it can be both quantified and qualified if we will—that damage has been done "to the hearts and minds" of the majority which, if we are not careful, may "unlikely ever be undone." It may well be that the majority group, unlike the Negro, was not disarmed physically, but he has most certainly been somewhat deranged psychologically; for how else would one explain adults spitting upon children, pushing lighted cigarettes into the ears of a diner sitting quietly at a lunch counter, or shooting a mailman peacefully walking his self-appointed round in the dead of night?

The heroic efforts being made to integrate public schools in New York City or New Rochelle; Gary, Indiana, or Englewood,

New Jersey; Mississippi or Georgia must first of all be clearly understood to be a part of a national movement on all fronts on the part of both Negroes and whites to undo this damage to both groups which in fact has been so long left undone. It is first of all a basic part of the struggle of the American Negro to secure the self-respect and dignity due him as a human being and as a creature of God. It is part of a basic fight whose battle cry, as Dr. Martin Luther King points out, is contained in three words: *All, here, now.*

The Negro seeks *all* of his rights. He seeks *all* of his rights *here*—in New York City, in Georgia, Alabama, Maine or California—wherever he may be. He seeks *all* of his rights *here* and he seeks them *now,* not tomorrow or next year or in ten years. He has waited long enough. He cannot and will not be a Job any longer.

Segregated schools, whether *de facto* or *de jure,* whether they provide equal educational facilities and high educational standards —indeed even if they were to provide the Negro child with a better education than that received by his white peer—would, in my view, still be unacceptable to the Negro in America today. They would be unacceptable because they symbolize, as do all other forms of segregation, the inferior and unequal status in which the Negro, simply because he is a Negro, is held by the white, simply because *he* is white.

The segregated school is but one of the many ways in and through which the one group is continuously reminded by the other that the first is inferior and the other superior. It also represents one of the means through which the Negro child is conditioned to recognize his "inferior" status and the white child conditioned to understand his "superior" one—for each must be carefully though subtly taught.

That this is the first and basic issue involved in the entire matter of school integration may very well be clear to most of those attending this conference—but it is not so clearly nor so broadly understood as it should be. In fact, it was the absence of any consideration of this point in Dr. James Conant's *Slums and Suburbs* that may have made many of us concerned with this crucial issue, fail to accord the book the serious attention it deserves.

For the Negro—indeed, for all Americans—there can never

be truly equal educational opportunities; there can never be an eradication of the damage done to the hearts and minds of both majority and minority groups until—and unless—each and every single and individual Negro is seen first of all as a human being, equal in dignity and potential to all human beings. He must first be judged and evaluated as an individual, solely on the basis of his ability and potential *as* an individual, and *not* on the basis of his being Negro.

I believe that in fighting against segregation, the Negro is fighting for his right to be a Negro. In fighting for his right to be a Negro, he fights for his right to *be,* for he can only be *as* a Negro. He cannot be anything else—nor should he be—or want to be— nor should anyone else want him to be otherwise.

In a multi-cultured democratic society such as ours, integration must not and cannot mean submerging or forgetting the specific content and values of one's own past, either as an individual or as a member of a group. In a multi-cultured democratic society such as ours, integration must mean:

(a) That we recognize and respect the differences among us; and, that difference means just that—different; it does not mean that the factor of being different makes some people better and others worse. These values must be judged on the basis of individual ability and potential.

(b) That the right to be different must not be detrimental to the whole nor to those parts of the whole who may wish to or must (because of their visibility) remain different.

(c) That the whole cannot discriminate against an individual or a group because of the desire or need of that individual or group to remain affiliated with what they consider a special value.

In other words, integration is in fact the fulfillment of the American dream of unity without uniformity.

If I may be permitted a parenthetical note on the affairs of our country in our international dealings, the struggle for the survival of the democratic concept in today's world, in my view, may perhaps depend more upon our success with the issues involved in integration, as I have outlined them, than on any other single factor, for democracy cannot truly flourish unless there is a respect for and an appreciation of the worth, dignity, difference between men, and value of each individual man.

If I seem to belabor this point I do so for two reasons. First, because it cannot be said often enough; second, because only by keeping these factors clearly in mind can we understand what I am about to say relative to integration and the Puerto Ricans. In discussing the issues of integration in New York City schools, Negroes and Puerto Ricans are referred to constantly almost as if they were one and the same. They are not. Unlike the Negro, we Puerto Ricans are not a race. We are, at most, an ethnic group. As such, some of us are "white," some of us are "Negro," and some of us are so-called "mixed."

Puerto Rico was discovered by Christopher Columbus in the year 1493. It was settled by Juan Ponce de León, the first Puerto Rican migrant, in 1508. The island's original Indian population was rapidly overcome and soon disappeared as a seperate discernible ethnic group. With the virtual disappearance of the Arawak Indian as a source of labor, the Spaniards turned to Africa. From 1511 to 1530 some 1500 African slaves were brought into Puerto Rico. From 1530 to 1555, some 15,000 more slaves were brought to the Island.

The bloodline of the Puerto Rican comes from many sources. Its base is Spanish. There was some early mixture of Spanish with the few remaining Indian women, some of whom were concubines and others wives. Europeans from many lands came next as soldiers, adventurers, and pirates. In 1511 slaves began to arrive. The revolution of Toussaint L'Ouverture in Haiti drove many French families into Puerto Rico. The Louisiana Purchase in 1803 brought other hundreds of families to the Island.

Ruth Gruber, in her book, *Puerto Rico—Island of Promise,* writes:

The bloodstreams of all these migrants fused to make the Puerto Rican of today. He is not a Negro, although 20 percent of the population is Negro. He is not Indian, yet the golden skin, the high cheek-bones, the aquiline nose, the gentleness and hospitality of the Indian are a common trait all over the island. He is not a Spaniard, yet he may have the blond hair of Northern Spain or the pure white skin of Barcelona.

But these, at least to my mind, are but the superficial differences between the Puerto Rican and the Negro. The real differences come from other factors. They come from our experiences, our conditioning, and our history as a people.

In our history as a people we have never had what we call in the United States a "minority group." In Puerto Rico the only people who are called a "minority" are those members of the political parties that fail to win an election. Puerto Ricans, therefore, whether Negro, white, or mulatto, have not received the same conditioning in this regard as have both the American Negro and white.

This is not to imply that there is no prejudice among us Puerto Ricans. As members of the human race we, too, suffer from this disease. However, in our history as a people prejudice has been limited primarily to relations between individuals. In our history of more than 450 years, we have never had a broad scale system of institutionalized discrimination *de facto* or *de jure*.

Puerto Rico was the only area in the Caribbean where the Negro slave did not rebel against his master, for right from the beginning there was a strong movement to free first the Indian and then the Negro. Slavery was abolished finally in Puerto Rico in 1873, at which time only 4.2 per cent of the total population were slaves.

In 1812, of a total population of 150,426 the slave population totalled 17,536 Negroes, having remained substantially the same as in the year 1794. In addition to the 17,536 Negro slaves, there were also 12,872 free Negroes living in Puerto Rico.[1]

Puerto Ricans, whether Negro or white, have never had to bear the horrendous burden of having to fight those who would make them feel or believe that they were lesser human beings than others because of skin pigmentation—or for that matter, for any other reason.

There has never been a race riot in Puerto Rico.

Dr. Melvin Tumin of Princeton (and one of the discussants at this conference) and his colleague, Dr. Arnold Feldman of the University of Delaware, conducted a field study among 1,000 heads of households, scientifically selected from all social strata in

[1] United States War Department, Report on Puerto Rico Census, 1899 (U. S. Printing Office, Washington, D. C., 1900); *Diario Económico de Puerto Rico* (March 21, 1814), as quoted in *Historia de la Esclavitud Negra en Puerto Rico* by Luis M. Díaz Soler, published by the University of Puerto Rico.

Puerto Rico. Their trained interviewers classified these 1,000 heads of households as follows: 608 white, 307 mulatto, and 80 Negro. On the other hand, the respondents classified themselves thus: 537 white, 397 mulatto, and 55 Negro!

"The evidence," say Tumin and Feldman, "urges us to the conclusion that skin color is considerably less important in Puerto Rico than in the United States; that it is virtually of no significance whatsoever in many important areas of life; that the majority feel that people of darker color are not blocked from major opportunities by their color. . . ." There is no doubt that, as Tumin and Feldman point out, there are areas of problems around color in Puerto Rico. However, as they indicate, ". . . it is fair to say that color discrimination in Puerto Rico is a subtle and minor theme in Puerto Rican life."

This, then, is one of the major differences between the Negro and the Puerto Rican in the United States: That all Puerto Ricans are not colored, and that even among those who are, color is not a major issue in Puerto Rican life.

Another significant difference is that Puerto Ricans represent a whole, unlike the Negro, who represents a part or minority of a whole. For this reason, Puerto Ricans are accustomed to seeing other Puerto Ricans at work at all levels, from low-income farm workers to the rich landowners who hire them; from the teacher who teaches them to the Rector of the University; from the district political leader to the Governor, the members of his Cabinet, and all the members of the House and Senate.

I repeat:

The Puerto Rican by experience, conditioning, and history is not a member of a minority group. He is both a part of the whole, and the whole itself—despite existing differences of class and race.

The Puerto Rican parent of the Puerto Rican child in New York City schools—and, indeed, many of the children themselves —were in Puerto Rico accustomed to attending school or seeing others attend school where all in attendance are Puerto Rican. The child of the Negro parent has also attended all-Negro schools, but unlike the Negro, I do not believe any Puerto Rican ever gave thought to whether his schools were integrated or not.

In other words, in Puerto Rico the Puerto Rican in a "racial" sense has—and has had—*ALL* of his rights; he has—and has had

—all of his rights *HERE* (i.e., wherever he lived in all parts of the Island); and he has—and has had—them *NOW!* For almost four centuries the Puerto Rican has possessed what the Negro now is fighting to attain.

We are fully aware of the fact that we, upon arrival in New York City and elsewhere, are seen by our fellow citizens as another —a new—minority group. We are also aware of the fact that we are seen by our neighbors as being "non-white." Since the question of color has not been a major theme in our experience or our history, we at first paid little attention to this designation. However, we learned fast. We learned that in the States a new dimension had been added: the dimension of "color." We found that skin pigmentation could determine where we could live and work. In fact, many Puerto Ricans soon learned that color was only part of the restriction they were facing: They were rejected as soon as they identified themselves as Puerto Ricans. I recall vividly the almost traumatic shock of one blue-eyed "pure white" Puerto Rican (whose ancestors on both sides descended from a long line of titled, German nobles), when he came to grips with this problem. In applying for an apartment, he had been refused, because he was Puerto Rican!

We realize that prejudice and discrimination in America are not wholly a matter of color and race. They are a state of mind— a state of mind brought about (among other things) by fear, which in turn often engenders hate.

We therefore reject the designation of "non-white." We reject it not because those of us who are in fact non-white are in any way ashamed of being of color; we reject it because we reject the state of mind behind it which, in referring to us as "non-white," is really telling us that we are not equal to others—that we are "inferior." To accept their value, would be to become inferior. Human beings are only inferior to others when they acknowledge themselves to be so. In so acknowledging we reinforce the belief of those who consider themselves superior. This we will not do!

We will not do this not only because man's scientific knowledge has demonstrated that one group of humans is not superior to another; we will not do so because for us to do so would be to retard the fight for equality which is moving forward on all fronts everywhere in America today. For, as I indicated earlier, the struggle for school integration in New York City and elsewhere in America at *this* stage is "first of all a basic part of the struggle of the American Negro to secure the self-respect and dignity due him as a human being. . . ." This self-respect and this dignity in this sense have been ours for centuries. They are ours now in Puerto Rico (a part of the American union), and we insist on keeping them wherever we go.

How to do this—how to keep our self-respect and dignity as human beings both in our own eyes and in the eyes of our neighbors—is the real problem confronting us. It is from this point of view—the point of view of *keeping,* not *acquiring*—that *we* must deal with the problems of integration in schools.

We Puerto Ricans have joined, are joining, and will join in ever-growing numbers with our Negro neighbor and with all others who seek to eliminate segregation in schools and in every other walk of life. We do so because to us integrated living has not been a far distant goal—it has been our way of life! And, if we are to maintain this way of life—and yes, eradicate whatever vestiges of prejudice and discrimination yet remain with us—we must *promote* our way of life. The realization of this is being pressed upon more and more of us. As a result more and more of us will participate more actively in promoting and maintaining that which up to now we had taken for granted.

We believe there *is* a distinction between the significance of a Puerto Rican child attending a school in which most or all of the children are of Puerto Rican background and of a Negro child attending a school in which most or all of the children are Negro. From a "racial" point of view, the all-Negro school is in fact completely segregated. On the other hand, because of the racial background of the Puerto Rican child, an all-Puerto Rican school may well be, from a "racial" point of view, the most integrated of schools. The real difference, however, is that the Negro feels that he is segregated because of his race (as, in fact, he is in most instances), while the Puerto Rican by and large does not feel this.

However, we have said that segregation and discrimination, particularly in the North, is more a state of mind and emotion than a matter of race.

Therefore, we recognize that the effect of the segregated school on the Puerto Rican child and on the Negro child is to a high degree almost identical when measured by the final result of their education, their achievement scores and reading level. We also recognize that this type of school and the present values that create and maintain it indeed generate a feeling of inferiority as to our status in the community which certainly affects the hearts and minds of our children.

At this time the Negro and Puerto Rican child both—even if for different reasons—by and large are not accepted into the middle-class society or its schools. They are excluded. Their education is a different one, geared to a different product from the education of the children who are members of the middle-class society.

Ours are the children of the outside group, and as such they are dealt with in our educational processes. Their occupational opportunities are considered to be limited, and these limitations are the framework of the educational process especially prepared for them. They are the "unfortunate" in our society, and the well-meaning teacher, not to speak of the prejudiced teacher, wants to help them to go through school with as few problems as possible, prepared to accept willingly the menial jobs which may be waiting for them and which many conclude a priori to be their lot.

The Negro today militantly refuses to accept this situation any longer. The Puerto Rican, not having the experience or conditioning of the Negro in this type of situation, has for some years lived in blissful ignorance—a dupe of circumstances. For, although Puerto Ricans were recorded as far back as the 1910 census as living in 39 states, the majority of the some 800,000 of us living in the United States today have lived here less than 20 years.

Actually, as we look back we discover that in 1940, although there were over 70,000 Puerto Ricans living in the States, mostly in New York City, there was at that time no "Puerto Rican problem."

It was not until after 1946 that we became a "race," that an identifiable descriptive stereotype had been created for us. In 1954 we discovered that our children, along with Negro children, were being described as "X" children who attended "X" schools. There also were some other children who were called "Y" children and they attended "Y" schools.

We also learned at that time that, when the "X" schools were compared with the "Y" schools, it was discovered that the "X" school buildings were older and somewhat less well equipped than the "Y" school buildings; also, that there were fewer regular teachers in the "X" schools. That is, that a disproportionately high percentage of the teachers teaching in the "X" schools as compared with the teachers of the "Y" school were teachers who for a variety of reasons did not meet the minimum standards established by the Board of Education for licensing a teacher—a prerequisite for becoming a regular teacher.

We also learned that the children in the "X" schools were not "achieving" at a par with the children of the "Y" schools. And, we suddenly realized that many of these "X" children were *our* children. With this realization came awareness of the segregated school and the fact that we could ignore neither its meaning nor its result. Thus, too, New York City realized that it could no longer ignore what a number of concerned citizens, most of them Negroes, had been aware of for many years—namely that New York City had many *de facto* segregated schools.

I realize that this description may be thought of by some as being either facetious or cynical, or both. I assure you I mean to be neither. I am simply trying to describe in words the awakening process of a group of people whose entire history and experience left them without the necessary "malicia," as we say in Spanish, to see what was happening before their eyes or to fully understand the implications and meaning of what they did see.

I am trying to explain to those who wonder, why the Puerto Rican has not been as militantly concerned as has the Negro over the problems and issues of integration and the segregated school. The Puerto Rican's experience, conditioning and history have made him slow to realize the threat and danger that segregation poses not only for his children but for his very way of life. The irony of it all is, of course, obvious. The experience, conditioning, and history of the Puerto Rican which has resulted in a way of life that has made him unable to perceive as quickly and clearly as he should have, what was and is happening to him, is the very way of life we here in the states seek in the struggle against segregation!

But much has happened since 1954. The symbols "X" and "Y" used in a scientific study are rather impersonal, as they should be and are intended to be. However, when the symbol "X" school is changed to read first "problem" school, then "difficult" school, and now "subject" school, we leave the realm of the impersonal and become quite personal and very understandable. Thus we now clearly understand that "problem" school—"difficult" school—"subject" school really means problem children—difficult children—subject children. And many of the children thus being described are ours. As parents we know some of our children *are* "problems" and *are* "difficult." But, are *all* of our children problems? Are they all difficult? This we would find hard to believe—and indeed we are assured by teachers and other educational authorities that they are not. We are assured that there is no intent to label, belittle, or stigmatize our children when these school designations are made. But, intended or not, we have now reached the point where we must begin to question seriously not necessarily the intention—for if it were bad intent, bad as that would be, we could at least understand—but the appalling lack of sensitivity, understanding, or perception on the part of those responsible for devising such names which is beyond comprehension. Children attending schools with pathological labels are labeled and marred; this is not good for children, it is not good education, and it is not good for education.

Yes, much has happened to us and to our understanding of the issues involved since 1954. Today we are able to say—and do say—that this type of labeling of the children attending specific schools in specific areas, whether intended or not, is another way of differentiating minority group children from majority group children, and is another means of re-enforcing the concepts of group superiority and inferiority. This is racism—as a state of mind—in its most damaging and subtle form.

Puerto Ricans are particularly adept at devising nicknames—"apodos," we call them in Spanish. Some of these "apodos" are so obviously descriptive of the peculiarities of the individual being so baptized that I say, perhaps not altogether facetiously, that this may be one of the as yet unknown and unmeasured motivations for migration.

Pitirim Sorokin in his monumental work, *The Fluctuation of the Arts,* describes, if I remember correctly, how different art forms are dominant in a given culture at a given time. In Puerto Rico the most highly developed art form has been, and no doubt still is, poetry. To be poetical one must, among other things, possess a feeling for words and their nuances, as well as the ability to verbalize concepts. There may be those who might say that this is the reason for our concern over names. They may also feel that this is why we are also greatly concerned over the current set of all encompassing slogans such as "culturally deprived," "socially disadvantaged," or the "culture of poverty." It may be, but I think not, because many non-Puerto Ricans are also concerned over the implication inherent in these pseudo-social scientific terms. In fact, many of those who use them admit they do not really mean what they suggest.

I ask: *Is* a culture that has for four centuries been able to maintain the individual dignity, value, and worth of all its members (despite differences in race and class) a deprived or disadvantaged culture when compared with one that has been striving to achieve these values and has as yet not been able to do so?

If it is a disadvantaged and deprived culture, it can only be so judged if the values used to "measure" it are values which support the concept of segregation—of the superiority and inferiority among and between groups of men.

If this *is* the value to be used in judging which culture is deprived and which is not, then let us come forth and say so clearly and openly. If it is not—and I know all here would agree it is not —then let not the educators or the social scientists be guilty of appearing to believe it *is* by creating, adopting, promoting and defending concepts and theories which in fact do reenforce the notion of the superiority of one group and the inferiority of another.

But you insist this is not what is meant when it is said that Puerto Ricans are culturally deprived. What is meant is that because of his background he is not properly motivated to take advantage of those things in our society which will enable him to raise his standards in life.

Here there are many questions I would ask if time permitted. I will ask just a few.

Are we sure that a culture that puts more value on status, prestige, symbols, and material possession, that makes of material things an end in and of themselves rather than a means to an end, a culture which in fact recognizes the great need to change some of its present basic values, is this a culture to be emulated so that in so doing we continue to perpetuate that which many agree needs be changed?

Is the child of a minority group culturally deprived because the majority group has established norms which *a priori* assume that most of the minority group members will not be able to attain the majority values, position, or education, and which proceeds to prove this hypothesis by providing a school system which is by and large geared to prevent him from achieving middle class majority levels?

I am aware of what those who talk about the problems of the "culturally deprived," of the "socially disadvantaged" are trying to say and point up. However, while I am not a semanticist, I believe that in the emotionally charged atmosphere of today's struggle for integration the use of what I have already termed pseudo-social scientific terms filled with ambiguities can only lead to the raising of questions like those I have raised and many more I could raise which, while of great importance, address themselves only to part of the problem. Discharging emotionally and value laden words into an emotionally charged atmosphere will most certainly result in thunder. At best, we can expect only an occasional flash of heat lightning. What we need is a constant bright light.

As we Puerto Ricans look at the total problem of school integration and equal educational opportunities for all, we are only too aware of the vastness of the problem. As a people with a culture, with history and with an experience we do what others do—we seek answers to present problems by falling upon our experience of the past.

In Puerto Rico proper, we Puerto Ricans have a living functional reality of the "proof," if you will, of our ability to both achieve and attain. "Operation Bootstrap" the program developed by the people of Puerto Rico to pull themselves out of a 19th century existence into a 20th century reality is known round the world. Thousands of people from over 112 nations have come and are still coming to see how we do it—to help us—and to learn from us.

It is the brothers and sisters, fathers and mothers, sons and daughters, cousins and the former neighbors in Puerto Rico of the Puerto Ricans in New York, and indeed many of the New York

Puerto Ricans themselves, who are responsible for this achievement.

If time permitted, we could also dwell on "Operation Commonwealth" through which the people of Puerto Rico are hard at work on one of their most difficult of problems—namely the development of a new and creative political status.

We could also discuss another bold conception of the people of Puerto Rico "Operation Serenity." Simply put, Operation Serenity represents the attempts of a people to husband their expanding economy, its means of production as well as its products in such a way that these means remain means and not become ends in and of themselves. In other words, the tools of society should remain just tools and man must remain the master not become the slave of his tools. Only in this way can man remain conscious of the value of man and not superimpose and give greater value to the things man produces.

But because of time we can only give passing mention to these areas. But, we remind you that we have this experience to fall back on as we look for a solution to our present problems. And, I repeat, we recognize only too well the enormity of our educational problems; after all, we are one of its main victims.

Nevertheless, we recall that against tremendous odds we in Puerto Rico are well on the way toward resolving our educational problems—as much as man can ever resolve these.

In Puerto Rico just 65 years ago only one Puerto Rican in every 41 attended school. 80 per cent of the population was illiterate—there were only 600 teachers. Some 40 years later in 1940 with twice the population we had 286,113 students attending schools even though many of the schools were dilapidated. But we still did not have enough schools for all of our children. By 1960 almost all of our grade school children were in schools; in fact, over 700,000 persons are receiving some kind of education in Puerto Rico today!

We now have almost 15,000 teachers. By the end of this, what we have termed the decade of education, we will have acquired an educational system equal to any.

We function from the belief that no one knows the potential of any child until that child is given every opportunity to develop whatever ability he may have. We therefore set out to provide for each child the highest education possible. We are fully aware that there are individual differences between and among children and that each will develop according to these differences; but we start out by affording to each child the maximum of opportunities we are able to provide. We do not decide *a priori* which child or group of children should or should not receive these benefits. They are available to all.

If it is new concepts that we seek in order to solve our serious and pressing educational problems, we should begin by assuming that each child, given every opportunity, will in fact develop to his full personal ability. If any doubt exists, it does not exist in the minds of the young people—it exists only in the minds of adults.

Can there be doubt when we think of the young American Negro of today, a product of a so-called socially deprived culture, the product of the culture of poverty, who has taken his destiny into his own hands and is staging one of the most profound and significant social revolutions ever seen in the United States?

In carrying out this revolution he has adapted a technique which, while conceived by the American Thoreau, was put into practice only in Africa and India. This technique, based upon the concept of nonviolence, fortified with love, requires the highest type of motivation and the most stringent self-imposed discipline.

Can we possibly say that there is no hope for the Negro youth of America in the face of all this, or must we admit that it is we who lost faith and lost hope?

As Governor Muñoz Marín of Puerto Rico once said in discussing the problem of developing the underdeveloped countries, ". . . in the final analysis, the great resource which must be tapped . . . is people. The great task is to unleash their creative energies, and the great first step is reached when they join together to work with enthusiasm and purpose, armed with adequate technical tools to achieve their own salvation."

It is this that the Negro youth of today is doing.

To quote Governor Muñoz again ". . . the great engines of creative energy in peoples are hope and pride . . . if you can find the touchstones to spur their hope and pride you will unleash their creative capacities and energies, and a new dynamism will enter into their lives before which even stubborn obstacles will fall."

School Integration: The School's Responsibility

John H. Niemeyer
President, Bank Street College of Education

I shall try to cover briefly in this paper four main points, or areas, of importance to our conference topic. These four are (1) A type of functional definition of, or my personal way of grasping, this thing called school integration. (2) What New York City public schools have been doing about school desegregation and integration. (3) Certain aspects of integration which lie beyond desegregation. (4) Some specific recommendations.

A Functional Definition of School Integration

I find it helpful in my own thinking about this problem to consider school integration as something which stands in contrast to alienation: on the one hand, alienation; on the other hand, integration. Now a school, it seems to me, supports alienation and obstructs integration when it does any or all of the following. *First, when it segregates children and youth by race, by social class, and perhaps by sex and special ability.* It is interesting to note that segregation by class, race, sex, and so forth "works" as long as a society provides distinct productive roles for the different groups and accepts these differences in roles as morally justified. This is the basis for the "hewers of wood and drawers of water" argument which we still hear used. However, the truth is that our society has been moving rapidly toward the time when we can neither make productive use of—nor accept as morally correct—the distinctly different roles brought about by organized alienation of particular groups in our society. Specialization we must have, it is true. But how early even that can begin without social damage would be debated among us. *Second, when it fails to educate to their true capacity lower social class children of special handicaps. Third, when it fails to develop a school world in which pupils and students who are characterized by social class and other differences*

61

can lead lives of individual achievement and develop a sense of belonging to a common endeavor, of being useful and respected members of the community; in short, when the school fails to provide for children and youth a living model of a society in which people of many differences can work and play together with mutual respect and with mutual, as well as individual, goals.

To repeat these three points in positive terms: We shall integrate our schools when we rid ourselves of segregation, learn to a reasonable degree to teach all children so that they can achieve up to their true capacity, and develop a school life which provides a positive social model for all children.

New York City's Accomplishments in Public School Integration

It is the school's responsibility to see that school integration takes place. I know, as all of us in this room do, that the school cannot do the job alone. Yet it can and must take responsibility for bringing about whatever changes are possible within the school system itself and for exciting every influence at its command to arouse the conscience of the community in support of the wide array of changes needed if the school is to move closer to the goal of integration.

At this, the closing hour of a splendid conference, I should like to suggest that the school system of New York City has in actuality set an admirable example of such an assumption of responsibility. Again, I know that an appalling amount of work still needs to be done. But I think it is important and reassuring for us to remind ourselves that New York City has already attacked the problems of school integration more than any other large city of the north; and in relative terms, perhaps more than any other community in the country. The full story of this will be told in an important report, "Public School Integration in the North," to be issued by the National Association of Intergroup Relations Officers. The chief authors of this report, Mr. Plaut, Prof. Wilkerson, and others, have played an important role in the development of this particular conference.

The New York City story can be told in brief as follows. In 1954, eight years ahead of any other city in the North, the Board of Education issued an unequivocal statement of policy establishing school integration as an official goal. In the same year it appointed a commission to study the situation and make recommendations for action. In 1957 it began an ethnic census of the schools. New York was the first city, or one of the first cities, to establish a post in the top administration to be responsible for guiding the process of desegregation and integration. There is hardly a device known to educators for achieving desegregation that the school system has not either used rather extensively or begun to explore on a pilot basis. It has used selection of sites, zoning, school reorganization, patterns of feeding children from elementary to junior high and from junior high to senior high, better utilization of plant, free transfers of pupils—and all of these in the interest of desegregation. The latter two devices are contained within the program which we call Open Enrollment. The system is also giving serious study, I believe, to the possibility of using the Greenburgh District-White Plains plan, or what is often referred to as the Princeton Plan. This is the plan for bringing about desegregation by having all of the classes on one, two, or three grades meet in one building. For example, K through two might meet in one building, grades three and four in another, grades five and six in still a third. This plan seems to be the most effective answer to the segregation problem in many smaller communities and I would think it of great usefulness in some of the fringe sections of New York City. But more about this and about desegregation when I come to my fourth section which I call Recommendations.

Beyond Desegregation: the Problem of Achievement

The third area I should like to discuss briefly is that important part of the process of school integration which lies beyond but, of course, is not unrelated to school desegregation. You will recall that a few minutes ago I said that we shall integrate our schools when we rid ourselves of segregation and when we can have all children achieve in accordance with their true potential and live together in a school in a socially positive manner. I am now talking about the latter two, which are really one, namely, the necessity for organizing the school for effective learning. If we attach meaning to the word achievement so that it includes competencies beyond the skills of reading and writing, however important these are, then I am saying that school integration demands that we go beyond the problem of desegregation and tackle the problem of under-achievement. We cannot avoid the fact that a frighteningly large number of children in the schools we are trying to desegregate move through school without developing the academic and social skills, or the personal and social attitudes and values, necessary for productive, meaningful lives. That there are exceptions does not negate this fact. For the large majority of these children, school, beginning with kindergarten, is an experience in pervasive failure. And yet, evidence continues to build up that many of these children who are considered as not having ability to learn do indeed have such ability. Furthermore, their parents, in spite of great problems and sometimes even degradation in their homes, do sincerely hope that school will mean a better life for their children. They would help their children learn in school if they only knew what to do. What is needed is for the school to conduct a realistic program to help them know how to do it. Am I saying then that our schools act on a belief that these children have a low learning potential, that our schools are not giving parents the kind of help they need in order to help their children learn in school? Yes, I'm afraid I am saying just that; although I know, and we all know, many teachers and administrators who are working on the under-achievement problem with deep sincerity.

In general, I believe there are two major weaknesses in the way we have been attacking this problem at the elementary school level. First, we have failed to place sufficient emphasis upon what are for most children the most decisive years of their school career, namely, kindergarten, first, and second grades. I am not opposed to experimenting with the nursery school years, in fact, Bank Street has a fifty-year commitment to the importance of exactly this. Nor do I have anything but admiration and enthusiasm for such programs as Higher Horizons. But by the time the children get to the third grade their attitudes toward the tasks of the school world and their attitudes about themselves as participants in that world are pretty firmly fixed. From that point on, for the most part, we face the problem of remediation. The second weakness is that few schools, it seems to me, have really thought through the reason that they should have a home-school communication program at all. Furthermore, they certainly have not set up machinery within the professional staff for working effectively with parents or even feeding back to the teachers the knowledge about parents and about the culture of the parent community which the specialists like the S.A.T.'s and often the principals possess. As far as the classroom or instructional program of the elementary school is concerned, will revolutionary changes be needed in order to solve the under-achievement problem? I would say yes and no. Yes, in the sense that obviously something different from what we are doing is called for; but, no, in the sense that the solution to the problem does not hinge upon the discovery of some new technique, some new knowledge which is going magically and suddenly to result in a so-called breakthrough. Of course we need to know more, vastly more, about the learning-teaching process. Of course we need improved books and teaching aids and more generous special services. But we also know enough right now, and we have the means right now, to do the job in the first years of schooling infinitely better than our school system or any school system is doing. What is demanded of us is to bring about changes within the school system—changes fundamentally in the concepts held by teachers, supervisors, and administrators regarding the professional role of the classroom teacher, the role of the principal, the role of the consultant, the role of the superintendent, and so forth.

I wish that we had a week-long workshop to open up the many facets of what ought to be changed and in which directions—and the even harder question of how to effect the long, hard process of change. But in these brief remarks this afternoon I can only ask the broad questions and assert that the need for change exists. Some of the suggestions I will make in a minute will be relevant to this matter. Let me at this moment say simply that I see two goals which any program of change would have in mind in our New York City schools. First is recognition by the school that these difficult learners can learn. These children have by the age of five already developed learning patterns, and the teachers' teaching job is to start where the children *are,* open up for them the exciting world of discovery and thought, and lead them on to new patterns of learning. Nothing revolutionary about that. The second is that the full weight of the school system should be aimed directly, and not just indirectly, at helping the teacher teach. I will have something to say on that a little bit later. The example of a good teacher, whose classroom I visited a few months ago, may help to point up the general instructional approach I am suggesting. This is a first grade teacher in a special services school in which 85 to 90 per cent of the children are minority group and lower social class. I happened to arrive at this school just as this teacher was returning by bus from a trip with her first grade class to what I think was the baby animal farm at Coney Island. I had been told that this teacher, in her second year of teaching, had been given the lowest ability grouping in the school. (It is well to remember that in most of our elementary schools children, at the age of five and one-half to six, when they finish kindergarten, are put into groups according to apparent ability—from the dumbest to the brightest.) When I saw these children pile out of the bus with their faces alight, their eyes shining, and their voices babbling, I would have said, "This teacher has one of the bright classes if not the brightest class in the school." I followed the class into their room. The first thing that struck my eyes as I walked around the room while the children were settling down to work, was the fact that all along the back wall, some pinned up and the others on tables so that children could read them, were books made by the children. It turned out that every child in that group had made at least three. Now this meant, as you know, that some of the children had written their names (with the N backwards!) and some children had written one or two words and some had written none and some more. But all or nearly all of the story told by each child had been written by the teacher into the book and the book was then illustrated by the child and bound in the way that children bind books in first grade. The first book I picked up told the story, it seems to me, of what I am trying to say about the importance of *starting* where children are, emphasizing learning, and having the whole school give support to what the teacher is doing. There was only one page inside the cover. The illustration showed what was obviously a man seated on a horse, and the story said "This is a cowboy. He's stopping for a beer." And as I read this I thought to myself, "Here clearly is a teacher who has already put wonder into the lives of these children. Equally clearly, she doesn't have a principal who says, as too many principals do, 'We have the bus for only a couple of days so don't use it on *that* class; they need to stay home and work on phonics. Use it on the bright class.' Also, this teacher accepts these children for whatever they are to start with. Barring one or two words, I am sure that there was nothing the child could have dictated about why the cowboy was stopping that the teacher would not have written down." We have to start with the vocabulary of the child. We have to start with the interests of the child. And of course it is not just a matter of our writing something down. It is what is inside us as teachers, our true acceptance and respect, that matters. The punchline of this story about a teacher is that, when I asked her—in February—how many of her 32 children she expected to be reading at grade level by the end of the year, she replied, "All but possibly two."

I must not take time to say more about the instructional program. Also, time will not permit my discussing the important problem of home-school communication in the interest of helping parents help their children learn in school. I might mention a study, the Teacher-Parent Communication Project, which has been completed in a school in the upper west side of Manhattan. This was an action-research effort to understand the problem of communication between the middle-class-oriented school and predominantly Negro-Puerto Rican working-class parents. Dr. Donald Horton of the Bank Street faculty, who is in the audience, headed this project, and I am sure that if you write to him next fall he will make the report of the project available.

Recommendations

I hope that I have emphasized the fact that we can all be very proud of what the New York City public school system has been able to accomplish and particularly of the movement we have been able to make in the direction of school desegregation and integration. However, that is looking at the water glass and exclaiming, "Good, it's half full!" I now want to call attention to the fact that the glass is half empty.

Much has been accomplished, much more will be accomplished if more members of the professional staffs of the school system will make deeper commitments to work to accomplish integration. I am not thinking of the persons—and we can be sure there are some—who really, in their hearts, oppose school integration. I am thinking of the multitude of teachers and administrators who are persons of good will, who believe in school integration as a goal, but who have not yet been willing to give this goal the priority which I should like to suggest it demands. I cannot state forcefully enough that the integration of our society—and for us school people that means responsibility for the integration of the schools—is the single most pressing challenge facing our democracy. We must meet that challenge or face dire consequences. And time is running out. Therefore let us face the problem with a sense of tremendous urgency. We must try to act wisely, of course. But we shall have to run some risks. There is no perfectly safe way to go about this job. The difficulties of bussing children, loss of the neighborhood school, the threat of parents moving to the suburbs, traffic dangers, and so forth: every one of our concerns will have to be faced with the question, "But which is the *greater* danger—this? or failure in school integration?" Now for my recommendations.

1. Desegregating Schools for Harlem Children

I frankly cannot see how, no matter what sense of urgency, what courage, or what wisdom motivates the New York City school system, the system can bring about desegregation of the schools in the vast ghetto of Harlem by simply accelerating "normal" desegregating procedures. (I use the word "ghetto" reluctantly because, although many residents of Harlem and scientists use the term, I think it highly inaccurate.) So far, all efforts have only affected the fringes of this community or given a small number of Harlem boys and girls—perhaps as many as 5 to 7 thousand— the opportunity to attend schools which are not 90% or more Negro-Puerto Rican. Outside of a vast bussing program, involving as many as perhaps 500,000 children being transported to schools each day, at an annual cost of at least $100,000,000, combined with an equally vast school construction program, I do not see how the school system can do more than expand the kind of program it now has started. With a determined effort many more thousands of children can be affected. But at best many of the Harlem schools will remain segregated until the housing pattern for Negroes is altered drastically. We must not underestimate, however, the importance to the Negro community of even such a stepped-up effort as a symbol of sincere movement toward integration in education.

My recommendation is that a responsible group composed of public school personnel as well as community representatives get to work to study intensively possible ways to solve the school segregation situation in Harlem—including the most drastic of all possible solutions. This, I suppose, would be to build schools outside Harlem and as quickly as possible close school buildings which are presently located in a way which insures, and will continue to insure, segregation; and then, provide the best network of transportation necessary to carry the children to these other schools. These would not be schools for Harlem children, but schools in many locations—some perhaps in clusters—to which children would be bussed from various parts of the city, Harlem included. Such a transportation system would be no different from that used for the children of those wealthy and/or well-educated families in the city who send their children to private schools and whose children go to school everyday by bus. How much would the construction program cost? How much would the transportation system cost? Would it all cost as much as a trip to the moon? Regardless of cost, the plan which would do the job should be presented to the public.

2. An Accelerated Transfer Program

Granting that the construction of new school clusters would take a great deal of time and huge sums of money, my second suggestion is much more immediately practical. The school system is considering the use of temporary structures. Let these be used to expand the facilities of schools which now have no more than 25% Negro-Puerto Rican enrollment *so as to create* under-utilized space for use in the open-enrollment program. A greatly accelerated program of transfers would thus be set into motion. It should be accompanied, however, by the following: (a) The full enrollment of transferred pupils in any school should be reached over a three year period and not more quickly unless small numbers are involved. (b) There should be a much more thorough preparation of both sending and receiving communities. For the sending communities this would include careful counselling with parents, advising some parents not to include their children in the program and others to do so. It would *not* wait for initiative from the parents. For the receiving community, preparation would include, among other things, workshops in which the practical problems would be discussed, plans for action made, and so forth. I know that some preparatory planning has been carried out by individual principals. But I would like to see this done in a more thorough and coordinated manner as a responsibility of the total school system. (c) There should be *absolute* compliance on the part of each receiving school with the instructions that the transferred pupils are to be distributed throughout the grades, are not to be dismissed early, are not in any way to be treated like temporary, or visiting, or intruding children. I know that the instructions to this effect went out to the schools, but there are too many examples where the instructions, for administrative reasons, were not carried out. This should be absolutely forbidden.

3. Use of the "Princeton Plan"

Recommendation number three I have already suggested above. It does seem to me that there are a number of fringe areas in the city where groups of administrators within the school system, perhaps at moments also joined by community leaders, should study the possibility of using the organizational scheme operating in the Greenburgh District of White Plains, commonly known as the Princeton Plan. Where there is any real mixture of populations in a community, this is a splendid way of achieving desegregation. There are problems of course. An older child may not be able to take a younger child to school, there may be traffic hazards for the young child, and so on. But what I am pleading for is that, no matter what the obstacle to desegregation is, we sit down and solve the problem which is the obstacle, not accept the fact that because there is a problem we will not be able to desegregate.

I said earlier that I know of at least one school superintendent who has been giving serious study to this particular type of organization.

4. Wider Community Involvement

My fourth recommendation I have suggested earlier, also. It is that in the expanded effort on the part of the school system to bring about desegregation and to foster integration, there be greater involvement of the grass roots community leaders: clergy, politicians, PTA, PA leaders, business men, newspaper editors, labor leaders, and so forth.

5. Supporting Teachers To Teach

My fifth recommendation is that perhaps the greatest yield in the attack upon the under-achievement problem could come from an appeal to the idealism and sense of worth of teachers. Teachers, I believe, do not want combat pay. But they want a sense that they are important, that they are worthwhile, that the difficult job they are trying to do is appreciated, that they are recognized, and that the whole school system exists to serve them. I might, parenthetically, say that we have never, so far as I know, had one of our Bank Street College graduates leave a teaching job in a "difficult" public school just because it was difficult. They have left because they felt that with all the difficulty and need there was so little social idealism exhibited in the schools. They have complained that there was so little support of the kind that they thought was needed. They want a principal's support for things that really matter in the teaching job. This is not the same as the principal's being a good fellow, being considerate when you are not feeling well, and believing that his greatest contribution is never to expect a teacher to stay one minute after 3 o'clock at a faculty meeting. These are the reasons we have had graduates leave difficult schools. But never because of pay and never because they did not want to tackle a tough assignment.

Now what do I mean when I say that teachers want to feel that the school system exists to support them? Here, those of you who are my very close friends in the audience and who are administrators in the public school system—may wish to reject me forever! I hope not. My impression, not just of the New York City public school system, but of many public school systems (in fact Bank Street is making some intensive studies in much smaller public school systems and we find something of the same pattern existing there) is that it is a pyramid with the teachers at the bottom and the pinnacle—meaning prestige as well as placement on a blackboard—being the superintendent—the top superintendent. And all eyes in the triangle look upward. Down somewhere below the triangle are children—in classrooms. I am exaggerating to try to make a point. An example of what I mean. Let us think of what happens to the teaching-learning process when the superintendent needs something—a bit of information; it may be a matter of life or death importance, or it may not be. He picks up the telephone—again I stylize—and calls the deputy. The deputy drops whatever he is doing and calls the associate. The associate, even if he is meeting with a group of parents at the moment and they are trying to work out a problem, drops whatever he is doing and calls the district superintendent. The district superintendent drops whatever he is doing and calls the principal. The principal, no matter what is going on in the school, drops whatever he is doing, and if he has a loudspeaker system he calls the classroom, or somebody goes down and interrupts the teacher. No matter what the teacher is doing, she drops it in order to give the information to the principal —and by the way, what she is doing is teaching children.

Now this is an exaggeration and yet I've lived enough in school systems to know that it represents truth. There are, of course, administrators who refuse to do this, or try to. I know of one principal who is pretty good at living up to the fact that unless the building is burning down he will not go into the teacher's classroom if she has put a sign on the door which the principal knows means, "I'm in the midst of something that I don't want interrupted." I know all of this, but the workings of the school system as a system actually do follow that other pattern. And I am suggesting that we will not really get the best out of teachers until teachers feel that all of this is turned upside down. In the *reverse* pyramid, the superintendent everyday is thinking, "What can I do to serve the deputy?" And the deputy is thinking, "What can I do to serve the associate?" And the associate is thinking, "What can I do to serve my 25 principals?" And the principal walks in every day thinking, "Now what is it that I can do today to serve the teaching needs of the teacher?" How to bring about the reversal, I do not know. Dr. Gross will undoubtedly be deeply concerned about this matter. To an important degree it is a matter of attitude. At every echelon individuals can do something about it if they will simply hold to the firm position that the instructional program for children is the purpose of the school and no other purpose must the school serve but that.

6. Recognition for a School's Achievement

My sixth recommendation is that ways should be found to reward schools which bring up their achievement so that they lose their "special service" rating. I have known one or two schools which have kept their special service rating even though they had improved beyond the point where they had a right to this rating. Maybe this goes on at the present. This is not enough, however. I wish that there could be the kind of drive to recognize achievement of all kinds, the development of real competencies in our schools, so that the most exciting thing that could happen in the superintendent's office and the mayor's office would be the report about such and such a school that has raised its achievement level along some dimension. I wish that we could constantly give recognition, that the community would know it, the teachers would be honored, the principals honored. I think that there is a good deal to be learned from the emphasis which Dr. Samuel Sheppard out in St. Louis places upon building up almost a football-rally spirit about, let us say, raising the reading level of fourth grades by one month! Every parent knows about it. Every storekeeper knows it. Every level of the school system knows it. I do not like to recommend a gold star approach, but nevertheless I wish that there were some way that we could capture the enthusiasm which seems to characterize Dr. Sheppard's program.

7. Intercultural Relations Program

My seventh recommendation is that I think the school system, as part of a modified and expanded in-service program, ought to institute intercultural relations workshops on a much more extensive scale. I recognize that there are intercultural relations workshops available to teachers. But I wish that our school system would place much greater emphasis upon this approach. We did a lot of this work in education back in the 1930's. Then our theory went beyond the 1930's level and we ceased to honor the approach rather than change it in line with the more sophisticated theory. I also wish that in selecting school principals and supervisors we would give great weight to a candidate's capacity to operate effectively in an intercultural situation. This would mean, I believe, more reliance upon the subjective judgment of a group of reasonable professional men as opposed to testing methods that can be scored on an IBM machine. I have the faith that such a procedure can avoid the danger of favoritism and other undesirable influences. Last summer we had at Bank Street a fascinating school integration workshop composed of interracial teams of teachers from El Paso, St. Louis, Louisville, and Charlotte, North Carolina. It was amazing to us how these sophisticated men and women, even from advanced communities like St. Louis and Louisville, had to learn somehow how to sit down and think together and face their emotions, their problems in this whole field. But they did it, and they did it in a way which was very exciting but which I cannot take the time to tell.

8. Let New York Find Talent—Anywhere

One of the shocking symbols before the alienated people of New York City is the small number of Negro and Puerto Rican teachers in our schools and the fact that at this moment there is not one Negro or Puerto Rican school principal in a school system in which 40 to 50% of the school population is Negro and Puerto Rican. This is mitigated by the fact that there are, I believe, more than a dozen Negroes or Puerto Ricans who are assistants to principals. Further, one of the deputy superintendents, one of the district superintendents, and a number of men and women in specialized, high administrative posts are Negro and Puerto Rican. And I should like to add at this point that all of these people have been appointed to their advanced positions because of superb ability and not for the purpose of symbol. But for most parents the only real figures of the power structure of the school are teachers and principals.

Again I would only raise the question about *priority*. If it is true—and it may not be—as I have been told, that there are not enough Negro and Puerto Rican qualified candidates for the principalships, and if at the same time this symbol is of such importance in the New York community, why doesn't the Board of Education go out across the nation and find some of the highly eligible Negro men and women and hire them for these posts. This would mean breaking the tradition that someone from the ranks deserves to be promoted (and in general I like these traditions), but again I must remind us that we are facing problems of priority, problems of priority in terms of various dangers. We should not stop because of the appointment system or anything else if there are ways of closing these gaps which permit so much ill will and negative action to pour through from people and groups into the body social and the body politic.

*　*　*　*

In offering these eight suggestions I have not meant to present a comprehensive program about integration or desegregation in our schools: actually all I have attempted is to suggest, in practical terms, what I mean by attacking the problem with a greater sense of urgency, of not being afraid to consider a break with established practices and modes of thought if doing this will lead us closer to a goal of such importance—the goal of desegregating our schools in New York City and bringing us closer to true school integration.

problems of priority in terms of various dangers. We should not stop because of the appointment system or anything else if there are ways of closing these gaps which permit so much ill will and negative action to pour through from people and groups into the body social and the body politic.

In offering these eight suggestions I have not meant to present a comprehensive program about integration, or desegregation in our schools; actually all I have attempted is to suggest, in practical terms, what I mean by attacking the problem with a greater sense of urgency, of not being afraid to consider a break with established practices and modes of thought in doing this will lead us closer to a goal of such importance—the goal of desegregating our schools in New York City and bringing us closer to true school integration.

Integration in New York City Schools: What, When, How?

Gertrude Noar
National Director of Education
Anti-Defamation League of B'nai B'rith

The conference began six months before when the Planning Committee first met. Theirs was a most difficult task—to think beyond the usual, to create a purpose with which very diverse individuals could identify, to inspire people sufficiently with the idea to make them part with money, and to allocate and assume responsibilities for the thousand and one details and tasks that were required to bring their plans to fruition.

The afternoon and evening before the opening session, the entire leadership team met for briefing. They reviewed goals and the way to achieve them, the dynamics of the group processes, the specifics of the roles to be played by chairmen, leaders and resource persons, and the mechanics of the reporting process. In order to insure good experience for participants, the leaders accepted for home reading numerous bulletins and reference pamphlets. Their preparation paid dividends when the very heterogeneous groups assembled and quickly got down to the business of carrying out the plans the leaders enunciated with clarity: The first objective to be attained, said the Planning Committee, was formulation of a concept of integration upon which policy can be developed. That done, principles were to be stated and finally recommendations were to be drawn up for processes and techniques to implement the policy and principles. While recognizing that integration involves the entire society, the Committee decided that all efforts in *this* conference were to be focused on education in New York City—including preparation and inservice training of teachers. To secure this participants, with few exceptions, were drawn from New York City.

Plans for the conference included a follow-up study of specific recommendations to be received from discussion groups and publication of proceedings which will include the major speeches.

Tribute is due to the seriousness and skill with which the leadership teams accepted and carried out their responsibilities. Who were the participants? One hundred twenty-five people registered and this probably did not include some of those presiding at general sessions and the speakers: Fifteen different colleges and universities, twelve human relations agencies, ten educational groups outside of the schools, two youth-serving agencies, four governmental departments, one labor union, one financial group (Ford Foundation), a number of elementary, junior and senior high schools, several administrative departments of the school system, the Bureau of Child Guidance and the State Department of Education—truly an admirable representation of many hundreds of thousands of New York's children and adults.

The first general session was opened by Harold Schiff of the Anti-Defamation League, who pointed to the uniqueness of the large number of cooperating groups. Mr. Edward Lewis, executive director of the Urban League of Greater New York, greeted the participants. He recalled the creation of a committee of 30 cooperating agencies that kept the problem of integration alive and noted that all of them were present in this conference. He spoke with pleasure of the cooperation of the school board and the school system. Mr. Lewis complimented the school system on the plan for integration already on paper. He expressed the hope that this conference would move the city closer to implementation of that plan.

Dr. Gordon Klopf of Teachers College, Co-chairman of the Planning Committee, presented the purposes of the conference which grew primarily out of the anxieties of many persons. Their concerns centered on the concept of integrated education. To secure it, mature, integrated persons are needed who know themselves and also know and are aware of the implications of our kind of society. Dr. Klopf expressed the hope that among the outcomes to be hoped for are more cooperation among agencies, more community support, more pilot projects, and hopefully the extension of successful projects to all schools. Recognizing the struggle that goes into all efforts, Dr. Klopf quoted Goethe: "He only earns his freedom and existence who daily conquers them anew."

The first speaker was Dr. Dan Thompson of Howard University, who presented a most insightful paper on *Our Wasted Potential: The Needs and Aspirations of Negroes From the Lower Class.* Some highlights follow:

Our future and survival will be determined in large measure by the development of our human potential. According to Toynbee, the great civilizations declined and fell because they allowed their youth to deteriorate. This points to the necessity of turning our attention to our youth.

The gap between white and Negro school pupils indicates that the talents of Negro youth are not recognized or used. To continue to fail them threatens our survival. Dropout rate, crime, illegitimacy and unemployment are from two to five times higher for Negroes than whites. Dr. Thompson spelled out some basic social facts. He said that all human behavior is learned. Motivation is the desire for new experience, security, response, and recognition.

Seventy per cent of Negro youth in New York City are lower class. Parents give little thought to planning for them. Negro boys especially are wasted. He described the culturally impoverished home in one-half of which, one or both parents are alcoholic, mentally ill, or criminal. The culturally impoverished parents do not know what the child is doing in school. Nearly all the homes, like the neighborhood, are ugly—no flowers, books or toys, no place to study. Therefore the children do not appreciate a beautiful school. One-quarter of the children are illegitimate. Many not wanted. There is little evidence of family pride and love. These families are dominated by the mother who is the earner. They do not plan for the future or teach children to aspire beyond a low status occupation. The adults have no conception of success in the traditional American concept. There are no bedtime stories about heroes. There is much chronic illness and the sick are kept in the home instead of in the hospital. Many of the adults experience imprisonment, separation, poverty. The children usually like their parents. Not all lower class children are alike.

Dr. Thompson described the social worlds in which Negro children live: *The matriarchal world* has existed for hundreds of years. There were no marriages in slavery and fathers were sold. This accentuates the female principle. The nice boy, to the mother, is like his sister. The male is hated and disturbed. The boy retreats from home and joins the gang which is a world of boys who distrust the matriarch, who believe women want only to exploit them. To be accepted by the gang one must be tough enough to reject the female principle and must then escape from the female school.

The marginal world. The children have shifted from one place, one family, one identity to another. They often change their names to the mother's current man. (Police call these names aliases.) No one ever tells a child he is beautiful, handsome, bright. Some do not know, psychologically, whether they are boys or girls. They are haunted by the question, "Am I really a man" and try to prove it with women, crime, and sports.

In the *nuclear world* the family is bound closely together to keep out others of whom they are suspicious. They are touchy about the children and how the school treats them. They have stable identities and stable relations at home. Teacher can't convince the children that she feels like a mother toward them. They and their parents give white teachers problems at the slightest sign of rejection or reproof. The world seems hostile to them. The structure of white society is opposite from the structure of Negro society and the school stresses values to which Negro children are not exposed.

How successful can racial integration be when Negro children are so deprived? There are one million of them in New York City and they are steadily coming in. The schools from which they come are not good enough to prepare the children for the New York City kind of competition. How can we take deprived children which the white school calls invaders and make good citizens out of them? Several approaches are used:

(1) The three-track plan predicts future capabilities when the child is nine. However, I.Q.'s and motivations can be increased. This is a self-fulfilling prophecy. Moreover, we do not know what jobs will be available.

(2) Three types of schools are set up. One for the mentally superior, another for the average, and a third for the slow, below average. This plan has the same dangers as the track plan.

(3) Democratic education which needs more experimentation and foundation support. We must spend more money on the culturally deprived child who has the right to become something of his own choosing.

We must regard this problem as a national emergency. Total community involvement is needed. Teacher education is vital. Special training should include social work method and internship. America needs intelligent, expensive, educated planning to solve the problem. If teachers are given training, more pay and more recognition, they will stay in these schools.

The children need to know they are part of our history and society. They must see themselves in their textbooks. For this we may need to subsidize publication of textbooks.

In-service education must include contact in Negro churches, picnics, homes. The white child also needs a better image of himself and of the Negro child. The Negro mother is sure her child is not good enough to go to the white school. She thinks whites are all geniuses. The white child suspects the same things.

During the first work session, groups found it hard to narrow discussion of integration to the point where they could formulate a concept. After listening in, I tried it myself and came up with this one, which is more than a definition and has four parts. Integration is a state of being which exists when people of all kinds (racial, religious, ethnic, social class, sex, and age groups) recognize and accept themselves, their differences and the contributions they can and should make to the common good; when they realize that they have prejudices and tendencies to stereotypic thinking and are willing to subject these prejudgments and generalizations to reality testing; when they live according to the Bill of Rights and also require its implementation for all other American citizens; when they value human life and strive for the full and equal development of the unknown potentiality of every human being.

Integration in education, therefore, requires organization, curriculum content, methods and materials which will produce and support the four elements that characterize the state of being called integration.

Participants seemed to agree that physical placement of white and nonwhite pupils in the same school does not constitute integration and that differences other than race must also be considered. All groups included social class; a few mentioned religious differences; many included ability. This lighted up some dissatisfaction with the common practice of organizing high ability groups.

Changing neighborhoods, high turnover of pupils, and the

rapidity with which schools become resegregated were recognized as blocks to the desegregation process. One group specified that teams of representatives from schools and their communities will need to identify all the problems that confront them and set out all that could be done. Only then can they come to a decision as to which of those problems and corrective activities properly and possibly can be done by the school. The final step is to set up a plan for the very next semester. Evaluation and replanning would follow in due course.

To carry out such a project requires top administrative understanding, participation, and facilitation. For example, the superintendent and principal would have to agree to allow school time for faculty meetings and would have to provide resource persons. Of course, a faculty itself would have to be willing to spend time and effort on their own re-education.

In changing neighborhoods, instead of worrying about the fact that children are likely to move away, the teachers will have to see each day as a new chance for each youngster to learn something he needs and wants to know. After all, we also never know how long *any* child has to live—or to remain in society.

It was gratifying to hear so many people express their conviction that good education for the culturally deprived would be good education for all children. As I hear about the special projects going on around the country, I am impressed with the fact that the teachers in them are implementing the great principles developed in the 30's in the eight-year study and in the 40's in the 20 cities experiments in human relations. Those projects were lost because they did not reach out into other schools—they did not affect the whole school system.

What are the principles involved?

(1) Satisfaction of such basic human needs as acceptance, achievement, recognition and reward.

(2) Development of positive self-concepts which follows satisfaction of those needs.

(3) Release from anxiety which follows development of the ability to relate and to succeed.

(4) The immense importance of success which cannot be provided until mass instruction and the use of a single text are replaced by the use of many publications on a wide range of reading

levels, by the use of vicarious and direct learning experiences in addition to reading, and by diversity of instruction and assignments. If teachers, administrators, professors of education, parents and community agency representatives in New York City are really serious about this, they can all begin at once to practice and support this kind of education. It would mean, however, that less emphasis would be placed on so-called basic education and traditional methods. The methods and materials are available. The sincere desire for change is not so evident.

In the afternoon discussions, emphasis was placed on the need for support and participation of the principal in developing democratic relations among staff.

Money entered into most discussions. Raising money is a complex problem. The "public" is not unified and not likely to be on any proposal. Some will vote against a bond issue and/or federal aid unless desegregation is specified. Others will vote yes only if desegregation is omitted.

Demonstration projects were proposed, but they will not necessarily *insure* adoption of "good" education by all the people. Use of federal aid by "Mobilization for Youth" demonstrates that government, commercial agencies, and the school system working together can accomplish something. It includes tutoring, retraining dropouts, reading clinics, and work-study projects. Any demonstration must reach both below and above the level at which it occurs. For example, the St. Louis Banneker project has not decreased senior high dropout because the senior high teachers' expectations and willingness to change their programs and methods have not been affected.

It was pointed out that both pre- and in-service teacher education projects should include going into the children's homes (on stipend). This is pretty difficult at the lowest level. Any project involving desegregation needs to document the benefits to white children as was done in Louisville, Kentucky.

For 25 years we have talked about individualization of instruction. However, this requires reorganization of the school-time schedules, a different use of space, more and different materials, varied methods, and warm relationships.

A proposal was made in one group that to effect change it is necessary to articulate a position, inculcate a philosophy into teachers, provide courses in social anthropology and in sociology and set up mandatory inservice education programs. It was proposed that administrators support a move to "push principals into line" and to permit teachers to do so. It was also suggested that there be no discussion with parents as to whether they do or do not want change.

One participant suggested that segregated elementary schools could be left intact if efforts were made to prepare children for desegregation in secondary schools. Can Negro children be adequately prepared for integration in junior high if for twelve years of life they have known only Negroes? It seems highly unlikely. It was pointed out that white parents have to join with Negroes to secure improvements that Negroes have been unable to secure. This will be done only if their children are actually in the same unsatisfactory schools.

Participants agreed that those affected must be involved in planning for desegregation: staff, students, parents, community agencies and pressure groups. Moreover, staff, especially, has to be committed. The basic question with which some groups struggled is how to make up for experiential deficits. The answer seemed to be, first identify the lacks, then describe the methods to be used, and, finally, provide the teachers with the wherewithal.

Dr. Mel Tumin of Princeton made the second address. Among others, he raised the following questions: Can the potential of all children be developed under the present system of grade organization, of segregation by ability, of marking systems that require a single symbol to indicate such disparate and multiple things as growth, effort, accomplishment, cleanliness, promptness, obedience, and 40 other elements far different from what the child knows or can do? Traditional concepts of scope and sequence will have to be relinquished in favor of developing curriculum in terms of the needs of the child, the realities in the society of which he is a part, and the readiness or maturity level on which the child is presently functioning.

The speaker emphasized the fact that in America we take as a fundamental premise, indispensable to our vision of ourselves as a democratic society, that we owe every single young person the right to equally good, equally enduring education. On our success hinges what we do in the next several decades. Although we can hope to minimize the *destructive* aspects of the conflict which will ensue as we disturb old privileges, old habits and comforts, we cannot hope for a smooth, tranquil transition.

Every child must have his potentialities freed. To do this both his pre-school experience and the total social living context of the school will have to be altered.

Dr. Tumin refuted the idea that pouring money into segregated schools would produce the desired results or that securing the cream of the teaching staff for all-Negro schools would do the trick. By the fact of their segregated existence, children are made to believe they are undesirable and inferior.

The speaker identified learning difficulties and low levels of achievement as symptoms of the diseases of low horizons of aspiration, impairment of learning facilities, and withdrawal from normal social involvement. The cause of the diseases is the social system of prejudice and discrimination which operates through segregated neighborhoods, unemployment, and social exclusion. Dr. Tumin therefore decides that social engineering to get at the sources of unequal readiness for schooling has high educational relevance.

Dr. Tumin outlined in forceful terms the roles principal and teachers play in determining the attitudes of children to classmates different from themselves. He said that the teacher himself must be the living model of right behavior, the guardian of morals and democratic rights. To do the necessary job, however, he must be supported by general school policy.

The speaker then discussed changes which he believes must be made in the general structure of New York City public schools:

(1) Elimination of competitive grading and graded curricula.

(2) Elimination of the concept of failure as it now operates.

(3) Examination of the defects of "automatic promotion."

(4) Revolutionary increases in resources in order to provide the many more teachers and facilities which individualization of instruction requires.

(5) Upsurge in the quality of teachers and teacher training.

(6) The amount and quality of support teachers receive from supervisory and administrative personnel.

(7) The danger inherent in casting and operating schools in the role of talent scout agencies.

Dr. Tumin closed with the reminder: "As we go in this educational experiment, so goes the entire world. We cannot afford to fail."

Dr. Martin Deutsch of the Department of Psychiatry, New York Medical College, discussed the *Dimensions of the School's Role*. He said, in part, that many of the barriers are created by social class and caste. His generalizations about the realities of segregation and deprivation in our society were stated in such an exceptionally vital manner that each of them could become the basis for discussion by groups of lay citizens and professionals throughout the city.

In terms of the demands for equality and what that really means within the school itself, attitudes, values, materials, structures, and methods must change. Society itself, with the school as its most pervasive institution, has maintained inequality, second class citizenship, poverty and discrimination. Society itself then must be motivated to correct and to compensate for what has been done. The school itself must lead the drive for the changes within itself that are required to provide the enrichment which has been denied.

Specifics Dr. Deutsch mentioned included:

Early pre-kindergarten opportunities.

Upgrading kindergarten in the status hierarchy. Concentration there on development of positive self-image and identity through the use of toys, books, letters and conversation with adults.

Ungraded sequences.

Misuse of marks as rewards and punishments.

The dangers and limitations of I.Q. testing and consequent categorizing of children. (I.Q. is sensitive to modifications in the environment.)

The self-concept: the role played by the mirror and photographs.

The track system. Homogeneous grouping is a luxury we can't afford; integration is more important.

Other specifics of great importance discussed by Dr. Deutsch were:

Continual correction of speech and language interferes with a child's chance to communicate a meaningful idea and with getting the reward in response from the significant other—the teacher.

In a project what the *goals* are must be made clear. The steps to be taken must not be mistaken for the goals. There is danger in publicizing projects. They must be properly evaluated in order to know where and why failures occurred.

Investments in limited programs must be limited and not automatically defended. Changes must be based on culture of the people involved. Middle class values and ways are more functional in terms of success in our society.

Parents can be helped to understand what they should and can do to get children ready for schooling.

Denial or ignoring of color and ethnic characteristics confuses the child's self-image and self-identification.

Social class barriers have to be jumped.

The child must be helped to learn and to compete in the school setting.

Orientation to the future (aspiration level) and delay of satisfaction, early learned by middle class children, have to be taught also to culturally deprived children.

Mr. Joseph Monserrat, director, Department of Labor, Migration Division, Commonwealth of Puerto Rico, delivered a forceful address. He said that unlike other people who came here of their own free will, the Negro was forcibly broken away from his roots and was therefore disarmed physically and psychologically. Now, however, the Negro seeks *all* of his rights including his right to be a Negro.

The speaker emphasized the fact that Puerto Ricans are an ethnic group, not a race. He reviewed the island's history, said that no broad scale system of institutionalized discrimination is practiced there. Puerto Ricans, at home, are not members of a minority group, said Mr. Monserrat. Both there and here they have had *all* their rights. However here, they find that color often serves to determine where they may live and work.

The speaker said that Puerto Ricans reject the designation "nonwhite" and the idea of inferiority. The majority of the 800,000 Puerto Ricans in the U.S. who have lived here less than 20 years are now joining the Negroes to secure integration in education and as a way of life.

Mr. Monserrat spoke bitterly against the common practice of labeling schools as "problem" and "difficult" and of thereby belittling and stigmatizing the children who are placed in them. He questioned the intent, and appalling lack of sensitivity of those who devise such names and systems, calling it racism in its most damaging and subtle form.

Mr. Monserrat closed his address with an account of educational progress in Puerto Rico and with a quotation from Governor Muñoz: ". . . if you can find the touchstones to spur . . . hope and pride you will unleash . . . creative capacities and energies, and a new dynamism will enter [life] before which even stubborn obstacles will fall."

The discussion on the second day was centered on recommendations for policies and their implementation. Following are a few from the many which will be forwarded by the recorders:

(1) The Board of Education was asked to reissue its policy on the positive value and necessity for integration in education.

(2) The Board was asked to issue a policy statement on the use of parents, agencies, and other city resources in the classroom, to provide for enrichment, tutoring and the establishment of study facilities.

(3) A policy statement was requested in which the Board of Education stands committed to play a leadership role in getting community cooperation to secure by whatever means may be required, the money for the necessary educational programs.

(4) A policy statement on the subject of compensatory education is needed.

(5) Policy should be formulated that funds and services be allocated on the basis of needs.

(6) A policy statement is needed with reference to employment and advancement of more non-white personnel. This should also include maintenance of certification standards.

(7) A policy is needed which will call for conducting and implementing research studies to determine the effects of such educational practices as grouping which prolong or promote actual segregation within a school.

(8) Policy should require mandatory in-service education for all personnel.

(9) Policy should call for greater coordination and cooperation with teacher training institutions.

(10) Colleges were called on to adopt policy on the subject of preparing teachers for integration.

(11) The Board was asked to establish added means for more effective communication with community agencies and parents.

The following recommendations for implementation of policy were made:

(1) Expansion of the functions of the auxiliary teacher.

(2) Smaller pupil-teacher ratios.

(3) Establishment of demonstration projects.

(4) Interboro teacher exchanges with understanding that those involved will be returned to their original posts.

(5) Utilization of school facilities for pupils and parents beyond the hours set for the school day.

(6) It was urged that the Board of Education seriously study the findings of this conference, and call together the Planning Committee, leaders, and resource persons to amplify the report and assist in making plans for integration in education in New York City.

The final address, delivered by John Niemeyer, President of Bank Street College of Education, dealt with "the school's responsibility" for integration. He said that alienation results from segregation by race, social class, sex, and ability, none of which can be accepted and morally justified. The school supports alienation when it fails to teach all children so they can achieve their true capacities. Moreover, the school must provide an environment in which its pupils live together in a socially positive manner.

The speaker paid tribute to the New York City school system for its assumption of responsibility for bringing about changes and for arousing the conscience of the community in support of changes needed to accomplish integration. In support of this, he enumerated the many steps taken since 1954.

Dr. Niemeyer discussed the necessity of organizing the school for effective learning. Now, for many children, it provides an experience in pervasive failure. He urged that more emphasis be placed on the very early years in which negative attitudes about the self become fixed, and that more effective work be done with parents.

The speaker identified two goals toward which change must be directed:

(1) Recognition that difficult learners can learn.

(2) Aiming the full weight of the school system at helping the teacher to teach.

Dr. Niemeyer recommended that the goal of integration be given high priority by all teachers and principals because it is the single most pressing problem facing our democracy. However, he was deeply pessimistic about the problem presented by Harlem. He recommended building new schools outside the area and transporting children to them. It is essential that both the sending and receiving communities be prepared when children are transported. They must be distributed and integrated in all classrooms and activities.

Dr. Niemeyer regards the Greenburg District, White Plains, type of organization with favor. He also urged that community leaders become involved in greater efforts to foster integration. He made a strong plea for giving high prestige to the classroom teacher and for honoring them when their pupils show marked improvements.

Dr. Niemeyer recommended institution of intercultural relations workshops for teachers and of using as a criterion for selection of principals and supervisors, the capacity of the candidate to operate effectively in an intercultural situation.

Dr. Niemeyer's final recommendation was that the number of Negro and Puerto Rican principals be substantially increased.

What did the conference accomplish?

If participants lacked information about Negroes and/or culturally disadvantaged children, they got from the speakers facts, understanding, and insight.

If people came to tell other individuals what they think they ought to do about something related to integration in education, they secured ears and attention in the discussion groups.

If members came to put something in writing to be given to the Board of Education and the administrators of the school system, good secretaries will see to it that the recommendations go into the final report and reach the Board of Education and the superintendents.

If participants came to get instruction so that they can exercise their roles as leaders or representatives from organized groups or just as effective citizens, each must ask himself what does he intend to do next.

It is easy to place blame, easy to allocate responsibility, harder to accept blame and much harder to accept responsibility and to define a specific next step to be taken.

To get help with this final step, may I suggest that within ten days meetings of those who were here be set up on a job alike basis. The opportunity for action should not be allowed to slip by. People should not go away feeling satisfied with just a talk experience no matter how cathartic it may have been.

Each is an individual—not everybody but somebody, not all but *one*. One can't do everything. Each one can commit himself to action by saying "I, with the help of God, *will do* what I can do."

Play your several roles as change agents with pride and courage in order that the good life in the democratic tradition shall come through speedy evolution, rather than by revolution.

The time is later than you think. The urgency is upon us.

It is easy to place blame, easy to allocate responsibility, harder to accept blame and much harder to accept responsibility and to define a specific next step to be taken.

To get help with this final step, may I suggest that within ten days meetings of those who were here be set up on a job-alike basis. The opportunity for action should not be allowed to slip by. People should not go away feeling satisfied with just a talk experience no matter how cathartic it may have been.

Each is an individual—not everybody, but somebody, not all but one. One can do everything. Each one can commit himself to action by saying "I, with the help of God, will do what I can do."

Play your several roles or change names with pride and courage in order that the good life in the decent, tranquil tradition shall come through steady evolution, rather than by revolution.

The time is later than you think. The urgency is upon us.

II

Readings from *The Fire Next Time**
James Baldwin

To enable the participants to feel the urgency of integration
Mr. Lloyd Richards, theatre and film director, actor, and teacher,
read the following selections from James Baldwin's *The Fire Next
Time* at the conference dinner meeting.

Introductory remarks by Lloyd Richards

I had met James Baldwin previously through his works, but
I first met him face to face in the Variety Club in Philadelphia in
February, 1959. The Variety Club in Philadelphia is a place where
most of the theatre people who happen to be in Philadelphia with
tryouts of Broadway shows congregate after the performance for
relaxation and to share the miseries and triumphs that we are all
experiencing while trying to put a Broadway production together.

I was in Philadelphia, at that time, as the director of Lorraine
Hansberry's *A Raisin in the Sun,* which I was preparing for a
Broadway opening. And Baldwin was there at the same time as an
assistant to Elia Kazan who was then directing Tennessee Williams'
Sweet Bird of Youth. We met, and I had a very stimulating and
exciting evening talking with this writer for whom I already had
a tremendous respect.

At the time of this meeting I was going through a very significant experience in my own life and my career. I was witnessing

* Copyright 1962, 1963 by James Baldwin and used with the permission
of the publishers, The Dial Press.

the evolution of a phenomenon. We had opened *A Raisin in the Sun* in Philadelphia with a very small advance sale, and for the first few nights few people had purchased tickets to see the play. However, from the fourth evening on lines began to form at the box office and tickets for the play were at a premium. The remarkable thing was the great percentage of Negroes who were buying tickets for the legitimate theatre. This so amazed me that at times I would stand in the lobby during the day and observe the people purchasing tickets; many of them had never been to the theatre before, they were amazed at the high prices, they were surprised to learn that performances were not continuous, that they had to come back at 8:30. I was aware that for most of them, purchasing a ticket meant a sacrifice of some necessary item in the household budget—and yet they came.

I would sit in the audience at night thrilled at their comprehension and empathy for what was happening on the stage and trying to find a single basic reason for this reaction. It came to me in a line from the play to which the audience seemed to respond with overwhelming joy and deep understanding. It was when the Younger family was packing to move and Mama was making elaborate protective preparations to move her cherished plant. Her young daughter Beneatha asked her "Are you going to take that thing with us to the new house?" Mama replied "Uh huh." Beneatha said with incredulous disdain, "That raggety old thing?" and Mama replied simply, "It expresses me." That to me was the succinct statement of why so many Negro people had made and continue to make such an effort to see *A Raisin in the Sun*. The word had gone out and circulated through the Negro community that something was happening in the legitimate theatre that expressed us.

I, as a Negro, an artist, and an American vitally concerned that the American experiment in democracy reach its ultimate fulfillment, one step of which is true integration of all minorities into all aspects of American life, am deeply indebted to and inspired by the writings of James Baldwin. When he is provocative I understand him; when he is indignant, I rise with him; when he is demanding my voice is raised with his, and when he speaks with the insight and compassion for all people that he expresses through his book *The Fire Next Time* I am at one with him. I am proud of this opportunity to read these passages. . . . For you see, like Mama with her plant, he expresses me.

And if the word *integration* means anything, this is what it means: that we, with love, shall force our brothers to see themselves as they are, to cease fleeing from reality and begin to change it. For this is your home, my friend, do not be driven from it; great men have done great things here, and will again, and we can make America what America must become. It will be hard, James, but you come from sturdy, peasant stock, men who picked cotton and dammed rivers and built railroads, and, in the teeth of the most terrifying odds, achieved an unassailable and monumental dignity. You come from a long line of great poets, some of the greatest poets since Homer. One of them said, "The very time I thought I was lost, My dungeon shook and my chains fell off."

A bill is coming in that I fear America is not prepared to pay. "The problem of the twentieth century," wrote W. E. B. Du Bois around sixty years ago, "is the problem of the color line." A fearful and delicate problem, which compromises, when it does not corrupt, all the American efforts to build a better world—here, there, or anywhere. It is for this reason that everything white Americans think they believe in must now be reexamined. What one would not like to see again is the consolidation of peoples on the basis of their color. But as long as we in the West place on color the value that we do, we make it impossible for the great unwashed to consolidate themselves according to any other principle. Color is not a human or a personal reality; it is a political reality. But this is a distinction so extremely hard to make that the West has not been able to make it yet. And at the center of this dreadful storm, this vast confusion, stand the black people of this nation, who must now share the fate of a nation that has never accepted them, to which they were brought in chains. Well, if this is so, one has no choice but to do all in one's power to change that fate, and at no matter what risk—eviction, imprisonment, torture, death. For the sake of one's children, in order to minimize the bill that they must pay, one must be careful not to take refuge in any delusion—and the value placed on the color of the skin is always and everywhere and forever a delusion. I know that what I am asking is impossible. But in our time, as in every time, the impossible is the least that one can demand—and one is, after all, emboldened by the spectacle of human history in general, and American Negro history in particular, for it testifies to nothing less than the perpetual achievement of the impossible.

When I was very young, and was dealing with my buddies in those wine- and urine-stained hallways, something in me wondered, "What will happen to all that beauty?" For black people, though I am aware that some of us, black and white, do not know it yet, are very beautiful. And when I sat at Elijah's table and watched the baby, the women, and the men, and we talked about God's—or Allah's—vengeance, I wondered, when that vengeance was achieved. "What will happen to all that beauty then?" I could also see that the intransigence and ignorance of the white world might make that vengeance inevitable—a vengeance that does not really depend on, and cannot really be executed by, any person or organization, and that cannot be prevented by any police force or army: historical vengeance, a cosmic vengeance, based on the law that we recognize when we say, "Whatever goes up must come down." And here we are, at the center of the arc, trapped in the gaudiest, most valuable, and most improbable water wheel the world has ever seen. Everything now, we must assume, is in our hands; we have no right to assume otherwise. If we—and now I mean the relatively conscious whites and the relatively conscious blacks, who must, like lovers, insist on, or create, the consciousness of the others—do not falter in our duty now, we may be able, handful that we are, to end the racial nightmare, and achieve our country, and change the history of the world. If we do not now dare everything, the fulfillment of that prophecy, re-created from the Bible in song by a slave, is upon us: "God gave Noah the rainbow sign, No more water, the fire next time!"

III

Conference Recommendations
on Integrating Schools
in New York City

I. *A Concept of Integration for the New York City Public Schools*

Integration is a social process in an environment through which and in which individuals and groups of varying racial, ethnic, economic, and cultural backgrounds may develop mutual respect and cooperative relationships and realize their full potential not limited by racial, religious, or economic prejudice in their life activities.

Improvement of specific facilities and services in segregated schools while currently valuable and necessary are not to be considered at any stage a substitute for integrated education.

Integration in education is a dynamic process which is possible only in a heterogeneous school population. The integration process becomes effective in schools when educational experiences are deliberately designed to develop an understanding of all groups and to provide adequate opportunities for each individual to secure self-fulfillment, to learn all of the ways of society, and to develop productive relationships with others.

The school plays a major educational role in the realization of integration. It assumes responsibility for initiating and implementing changes in content of curriculum, instruction, materials, and school organization which will produce and support the elements that characterize the process of integration. Basic to and underlying all of the school's efforts is a full understanding of and a commitment to the concept of complete integration—involving the schools of Harlem and Bedford Stuyvesant as well as all other areas of the city—so that policies and programs will reflect a dynamic movement toward full realization of the ultimate goal.

II. *Conference Resolutions*

(1) The Board of Education should allocate a substantial part of its budget for a more comprehensive program of research and experimentation in guidance and instruction for individuals of varying cultural backgrounds, for effective approaches of intergroup education, and for evaluating administrative measures designed to promote integration.

(2) In recognition of the fact that the achievement of school and classroom integration requires the cooperation of several nonschool governmental agencies, the Board of Education should call upon the Mayor to establish a functioning Coordination Committee for School Integration. This Committee should consist of policy-level representatives of the Board of Education, the City Commission on Human Rights, the City Planning Commission, the N. Y. C. Housing Authority, the Housing and Redevelopment Board, and the Bureau of Real Estate. The Mayor should be urged to assure the effective functioning of this Committee and prepare a time schedule for implementing school integration.

(3) On the premise that an effective integrated public school system is essential to the economic growth of a community, the Board of Education should be more aggressive in interpreting the needs of public education to those segments of the community representing business and political interests, and in seeking their help to obtain adequate funds.

The Board should continue to promote the expansion of federal assistance programs already in operation in the schools, and the development of new programs, including funds for human relations and intergroup education.

The Board must intensify its efforts to enlist the support of the Mayor and other city officials, community leaders and organizations to obtain the massive financial resources required for the development of effective integrated education.

(4) The Board of Education should evaluate current instruc-

tional procedures and develop new and imaginative processes to implement the goal of complete school integration. For example, ability and other methods of grouping should be re-evaluated in terms of their effect upon integration; the desirability of extending the school day and the school year should be considered; and attention should be given to establishing adult education programs which are designed to give parents the understanding and the knowledge they need to further their children's education.

(5) The Board of Education should further develop and greatly extend its program for educating all school personnel in human development and social relations, emphasizing intercultural understandings and values. Participation in this program should be required. The program should be based upon sound theoretical concepts, and should deal with the real problems and needs of the New York City community. Members of the Board of Education should be involved directly in the planning and development of this in-service educational program.

(6) The Board of Education has publicly declared that its goal is to bring about true integration of schools. It is understood that the Board has formulated a comprehensive plan for achieving this goal.[1] This plan should now be announced. The plan should provide for the further development of programs now in operation and the introduction of new approaches. Among these, for example, consideration should be given to the development of conclaves of schools on all levels in educational centers located in park-like areas of the community, serving large numbers of children from various sections of the city;[2] the location of schools in diverse population "fringe" areas to provide for the deliberate development of integrated school populations from different groups in the city by site selection or dual-directional open enrollment; and the adaptation of some variation of the Princeton Plan where children are in schools organized by grade level rather than district.

III. *Conference Recommendations*

(1) *Community organizations and the family*
Second class citizenship has been imposed upon large seg-

---

[1] The recently announced Board of Education Plan is included in the Appendix.
[2] See Bibliography for reference.

ments of our population at various times in the history of our country, lasting for some groups more than 100 years. Measures must be taken to overcome educational handicaps of young people resulting from such social inequalities. The total social environment is a major factor affecting a child's capacity and thus his performance in school. If integration is really to take place, community organizations and the family must assume responsibility for creating a readiness for, an acceptance of and a commitment to integration.

The Conference Recommends that the Board of Education
    (a) Urge organizations and agencies to make a greater effort to pool and coordinate their activities to further integration in the schools, consulting these groups in advance on relevant policy decisions.
    (b) Accelerate its efforts to involve the organized community in minimizing the educationally undesirable effects of high family mobility.
    (c) Request that community agencies provide more meaningful community experience for teachers by making available their resources, facilities, and staff personnel.
    (d) Enlist the help of community organizations and communication media in doing needed research and disseminating information on existing data.

    (2) *Professional Personnel*
    Planned school integration calls for special emphasis on the preservice training, selection, assignment, and in-service training of professional personnel. Teachers and other professionals who function in sensitive and intimate association with children must have awareness and understanding of the needs and problems of children of varying racial, ethnic, and cultural backgrounds, as well as the required attitudes and teaching skills.
    Teachers, district administrators, and supervisors must understand that they are obligated to help implement the Board of Education's policy of integration, and should receive the Board's full support in their efforts to do so.
    Further, it must be recognized that planned integration calls for increased participation by minority-group persons—as teachers, supervisors, and administrators.

It is also necessary that institutions of higher education preparing school personnel keep abreast of and serve the changing needs of a city in transition.

The Conference Recommends that the Board of Education

(a) Urge schools of education to require their graduates to have adequate training in the history of minorities, cultural anthropology, and the behavioral sciences.

(b) Use its influence to have teacher education reflect a pattern of preparation which includes laboratory and course experiences designed to enable teachers to work effectively and sensitively with children from culturally different groups.

(c) Urge schools of education to assume a greater role in encouraging and recruiting more minority group persons to enter the profession.

(d) Seek to stimulate schools of education to undertake research directed toward developing effective procedures for coping with the special motivational and learning problems of children with socially induced educational handicaps.

(e) Review its policies and practices of recruiting and upgrading professional personnel so as to employ and advance more Negro, Puerto Rican, and other minority-group professionals.

(f) Formulate and implement a policy which assures the equitable distribution of staff with successful teaching experience as well as minority-group personnel among the schools of the city.

(g) Hold each field superintendent responsible for gathering and using information and resource material on intercultural relations and for implementing the policy of integration in the schools under his jurisdiction.

(h) Develop an exchange program for experienced teachers similar to the Puerto Rican exchange program, but involving the American South.

(3) *School Organization*

It is recognized that the fundamental purpose of education is to improve the life chance of each individual child, and educational programs to this end are the responsibility of the Board of Education. School organization must be consistent with this general purpose.

The Conference Recommends that the Board of Education
(a) Assume responsibility for preventing and resolving conflict regarding re-zoning.

(b) Consider the implications of recent research findings for the development of programs of pre-school education.

(c) Provide foster homes or other suitable residence for the 2 to 3 per cent of socially damaged children whose life at home is incompatible with profitable school experiences.

(d) Undertake to relieve the problems resulting from the high mobility of minority-group families by arranging for children who have moved to remain in the same school until the end of the year.

(4) *Curriculum and Instruction*
The school must have a curriculum which meets the needs of the people and considers the particular characteristics of New York City.

The Conference Recommends that the Board of Education
(a) Have teachers and schools utilize racial, religious, and ethnic dissimilarities to enrich the curriculum and to help the child identify with his own image in a positive way.

(b) Re-examine the curriculum to the end of providing emphasis on cognitive learning from the earliest year.

(c) Plan and implement counseling procedures which will encourage larger proportions of minority-group students to follow academic programs on the secondary level.

(d) Assure that professional personnel understand that, when given opportunity, large numbers of minority-group children who are achieving inadequately at a given time demonstrate the ability for higher achievement at a later stage in their development.

(e) Obtain and provide textbooks on all levels which give valid interpretations of the historical and contemporary roles in our society of different cultural groups, and which include accounts of individual persons with whom minority-group children can easily identify.

(f) Continue and expand the present program of cultural tours and trips.

(g) Insure that instruction be based upon effective means of communicating with children of culturally different backgrounds.

(5) *Special Services*

Integrated education requires special services. Guidance and psychological services, remedial and compensatory activities, and the Human Relations Unit must be expanded. The lessening of community tensions rests greatly with the Human Relations Unit. Identifying and defining the human relations needs of the school system is the responsibility of this Unit.

The Conference Recommends that the Board of Education

(a) Effect the expansion of the Human Relations Unit's personnel, program, and facilities.

(b) Assure that Assistant Superintendents consult with the Human Relations Unit for the prevention or resolution of difficult situations when they arise.

(c) Improve and expand guidance services in all schools. For example, as long as New York City maintains special high schools, special effort should be made to identify and develop talented minority-group children so they are able to take their place in any high school in the city. Counseling should be directed to this end.

(d) Improve and expand psychological services.

(e) Establish experimental projects such as study and cultural centers utilizing school facilities.

(6) *Research and Re-evaluation*

Completely integrated, equal, equally good education is a relatively new concept requiring profound changes which are not possible within the framework of the present school program. The re-evaluation of existing procedures and concepts and the institution of special experimental programs are vital transitional steps along the road to the ultimate goal.

The Conference Recommends that the Board of Education

(a) Continually re-evaluate its concept of integration so that it may be conceived as an evolving, dynamic process related to changing needs and conditions, and communicate this concept clearly and forcefully throughout the system.

(b) Urge the Board of Higher Education to examine city college entrance requirements to learn to what degree potential minority-group students have been excluded.

(5) Special Services

Integrated education requires special services: Guidance and psychological services, remedial and compensatory activities, and the Human Relations Unit must be expanded. The lessening of community tensions rests greatly with the Human Relations Unit. Identifying and defining the human relations needs of the school system is the responsibility of this Unit.

The Conference Recommends that the Board of Education

(a) Effect the expansion of the Human Relations Unit's personnel, program, and facilities.

(b) Assure that Assistant Superintendents consult with the Human Relations Unit for the prevention or resolution of difficult situations when they arise.

(c) Improve and expand guidance services in all schools. For example, as long as New York City maintains special high schools, special effort should be made to identify and develop talented minority-group children so they are able to take their place in any high school in the city. Counseling should be directed to this end.

(d) Improve and expand psychological services.

(e) Establish experimental projects such as study and cultural centers utilizing school facilities.

(6) Research and Re-evaluation

Complete a quicker, equal, equall, good education is a relatively new concept requiring profound changes which are not possible within the framework of the present school program. The re-evaluation of existing procedures, and concepts and the initiation of special experimental programs are vital transitional steps along the road to the ultimate goal.

The Conference Re-emphasizes that the should by Definition

(a) Continually re-evaluate its concept of integration so that it may be conceived as an evolving, dynamic process related to changing needs and conditions, and communicate this concept clearly and forcefully throughout the system.

(b) Urge the Board of Higher Education to examine city college entrance requirements to learn to what degree potential minority-group students have been excluded.

Appendix

Selected Bibliography

American Jewish Committee. *A Survey on School Integration in Northern Cities.* New York, 1957.

American Jewish Congress. *Statement of the American Jewish Congress on School Segregation, Northern Style,* Submitted to the House Committee on Education and Labor, March 29, 1962. New York, 1962.

Anderson, Margaret. "After Integration—Higher Horizons." *The New York Times Magazine,* April 21, 1963.

Bettelheim, Bruno. "Segregation: New Style." *School Review,* Autumn 1958.

Blumer, Herbert. "Social Science and the Desegregation Process." *The Annals,* March 1956.

Boucher, B. P., and H. C. Brooks. "School Integration and its Relation to the Distribution of Negroes in the United States Cities." *Education Forum,* January 1960.

Citizens Committee for Children of New York. "No Entiendes— Do You Understand?" *NE,* November 1961.

Clark, Dennis. "Desegregation, An Appraisal of Evidence." *Journal of Social Issues,* No. 4, 1953.

Clark, Kenneth. "Desegregation: Its Implications for Orthopsychiatry." *American Journal of Orthopsychiatry,* July 1956.

Cliff, Virgil A. "Does the Dewey Philosophy Have Implications for Desegregating Schools?" *Journal of Negro Education,* Winter 1960.

Commission on Civil Rights. *Conference Before the United States Commission on Civil Rights*—Fourth Annual Education Conference on Problems of Segregation and Desegregation of Public Schools, Washington, May 1962.

106

APPENDIX

Commission on Human Rights. *Questions and Quotes About School Integration and Your Child,* Cyril Tyson (Editor), New York City Commission on Human Rights, 1961.

Committee on Education and Labor. *Integration in Public Education Programs.* House of Representatives, United States Congress, 1962.

Dean, John P., and Alex Rosen. *A Manual of Intergroup Relations.* Chicago, University of Chicago Press, 1956.

"De Facto Segregation in the Chicago Public Schools." *Crisis,* February 1958.

Deutsch, Martin. *Minority Group and Class Status as Related to Social and Personality Factors in Scholastic Achievement.* Monograph No. 2, 1960. The Society for Applied Anthropology.

Dickrey, J. G. "Looking at Integration," *Educational Leadership,* Vol. 13, November 1955.

Dodson, Dan W. "The North, Too, Has Segregation Problems," *Educational Leadership,* November 1955.

Dodson, Dan W. "Power as a Dimension of Education," *Journal of Educational Sociology,* January 1962.

Dodson, Dan W. "Racial Integration: Some Principles and Procedures." *Journal of Educational Sociology,* October 1954.

The East Harlem Project. *Releasing Human Potential: A Study of East Harlem-Yorkville School Bus Transfer.* New York City Commission on Human Rights, August 1962.

Educational Policies Commission, *Education and the Disadvantaged American.* Washington, D.C., National Educational Association, 1962.

Fisher, J. H. "Can Segregated Schools Be Abolished?" *Journal of Negro Education,* Spring 1954.

Fountineel, E. "Built-in Segregation." *Commonweal,* April 7, 1961.

Furman, D. W. (Editor). *Integration: A Challenge and Opportunity for Education in the Middle States,* Annual Proceedings of the Mid-States Council for Social Studies. New York, Bank Street College of Education, 1957.

Garber, Lee O. "Neighborhood Attendance is no Longer a Legal Excuse for Racially Segregated Schools." *Nation's Schools,* November 1962.

Giles, Harry H. *The Integrated Classroom*. New York, Basic Books, 1959.

Glazer, Nathan. "Is Integration Possible in the New York City Schools?" *Commentary*, September 1960.

Goldblatt, Harold, and Cyril Tyson. *Some Self-Perceptions and Teacher Evaluations of Puerto Rican, Negro, and White Pupils in 4th, 5th, and 6th Grades (P.S. 198M)*, Research Report No. 12. The New York City Commission on Human Rights, October 1962.

Gregory, Francis A., *et al.* "From Desegregation to Integration in Education." *Journal of Intergroup Relations*, Winter 1962.

Groff, Patrick J. "Teacher Organizations and School Desegregation." *School and Society*, December 15, 1962.

Group for the Advancement of Psychiatry. *Psychiatric Aspects of School Desegregation*, Report No. 37, May 1957.

Hansen, Carl F. *Miracle of Social Adjustment: Desegregation in the Washington, D.C. Schools*. Anti-Defamation League of B'nai B'rith, 1957.

Hansen, Carl F. Addendum, *A Five-Year Report on Desegregation in the Washington, D.C. Schools*. Anti-Defamation League of B'nai B'rith, 1960.

Hansen, Carl F. "The Scholastic Performances of Negro and White Pupils in the Integrated Public Schools of the District of Columbia." *Harvard Educational Review*, Summer 1960.

Havighurst, Robert. "Social Urban Renewal and the Schools." *Integrated Education*, April 1963.

Hogan, Rev. William. "School Segregation Northern Style." *Community*, Chicago Friendship House, January 1962.

Holman, L. H. "How the Illinois NAACP Fights School Segregation." *Crisis*, May 1961.

Horton, Donald. "School Desegregation and Integration: Definition of Terms." New York, Bank Street College of Education, July 1959.

Hyram, George H. "Has Integration Worked at Saint Louis University?" *Interracial Review*, March 1960.

Illinois Commission on Human Relations. *The Integration of Public Schools in Illinois*. Chicago, 1959.

Klopf, Gordon. *Expanding Opportunities Through Guidance*. New York State Commission for Human Rights, 1961.

Knoll, E. "The Truth About Desegregation in the Washington, D.C. Public Schools." *Journal of Negro Education,* Spring 1959.

Laster, Israel A. *Elements of the New York Chapter Experience with School Integration in New York City.* American Jewish Committee, August 1962.

Laster, Israel A. *The Elimination of* De Facto *Segregation in the Public Schools in New York City.* American Jewish Committee, July 1961.

Laster, Israel A. *The Fallacy of the Neighborhood School Concept.* American Jewish Committee.

Levine, Daniel. "City Schools Today: Too Late with Too Little?" *Phi Delta Kappan,* November 1962.

Levine, Jacqueline. "Summary of 'Psychiatric Aspects of School Desegregation.' " A report issued by the Group for the Advancement of Psychiatry, 1951. American Jewish Congress.

Levine, Naomi, and Will Maslow. *From Color Blind to Color Conscious: A Study of Public School Integration in New York City.* American Jewish Congress, 1959.

Lewis, H., and Hill, M. "Desegregation, Integration and the Negro Community." *The Annals,* March 1956.

Lieberman, Myron. "Equality of Educational Opportunity." *Harvard Educational Review.* Summer 1959.

Lincoln, C. Erich. *Race Relations Handbook.* Anti-Defamation League, 1964. A source book for answering questions on race relations problems and attitudes in the United States.

Marquardt, William F. "Puerto Ricans and Inter-American Understanding." *The Journal of Educational Sociology.* Special Issue, May 1962.

Maslow, Will. "*De Facto* Public School Segregation." *Villanova Law Review,* Spring 1961.

Maslow, Will, and Richard Cohen. *School Segregation, Northern Style.* Public Affairs Pamphlet, 1961.

Maslow, Will. "Desegregation: The Northern Problem." *Teachers College Record,* October 1961.

Meyer, Gladys. *Parent Action in School Integration.* New York City, United Parents Association, 1961.

Morland, J. Kenneth. *Token Segregation and Beyond.* Atlanta,

Southern Regional Council; New York, Anti-Defamation League of B'nai B'rith, 1963.

"Negro Education in the United States." *Harvard Educational Review,* Special Issue, Summer 1960.

New York City Board of Education—Commission on Integration. *Toward Greater Opportunity.* June 1960.

New York State Commission on Human Rights. *Expanding Opportunities Through Guidance.* Conference for Guidance Workers, Glens Falls, New York, February 1961. Gordon J. Klopf, Chairman.

Noar, Gertrude. *Teaching and Learning the Democratic Way.* Englewood Cliffs, N.J., Prentice Hall, 1963.

Norman, A. "New Approach to Negro Education." *Journal of Negro Education,* Winter 1961.

Passow, A. Harry (Editor). *Education in Depressed Areas.* New York, Bureau of Publications, 1963.

Pettigrew, Thomas. *Epitaph for Jim Crow.* Anti-Defamation League, 1963.

Plaut, R. L. "Racial Integration in Higher Education in the North." *Journal of Negro Education,* Summer 1962.

Reid, Ira de A. "Integration: Ideal, Process and Situation." *Journal of Negro Education,* Summer 1954.

Reissman, Frank. *The Culturally Deprived Child.*

Rivlin, Harry. *Teachers for the Schools of Our Big Cities.* New York, City University, 1962.

Robinson, J. B. "De Facto Segregation in the Northern Public Schools; its Anatomy and Treatment." *Journal of Jewish Communal Service,* Fall 1962.

Schiff, Harold. *Human Relations in Education.* An In-Service Course Outline for Teachers in the New York City Schools. New York, Anti-Defamation League of B'nai B'rith, 1960.

Schiff, Harold. *Integration in the New York City Schools.* Paper presented at a hearing of the Committee on Education and Labor, Washington, D.C., March 1962. New York, Anti-Defamation League of B'nai B'rith, 1962.

Shagaloff, June. *Public School: Desegregation in the North and West, Memorandum.* New York, National Association for the Advancement of Colored People, January 1963.

Simon, P. "Let's Integrate our Teachers." *Christian Century,* February 20, 1957.

Smith, Benjamin F. "Racial Integration in Public Education": An Annotated Bibliography, Part IV. *Negro Educational Review,* January 1963.

Society For The Psychological Study of Social Issues. *The Role of the Social Sciences in Desegregation: A Symposium.* Anti-Defamation League of B'nai B'rith, August 1958.

Southern School News. "Integration and Desegregation Have Different and Distinctive Meanings." *Southern School News,* March 1961.

Stallings, Frank H. *Atlanta and Washington—Racial Differences in Academic Achievement.* Atlanta, Southern Regional Council, February 26, 1960.

Status of the Public School Education of Negro and Puerto Rican Children in New York City. New York City, Public Education Association, October 1955.

Teachers for Integrated Schools, Chicago, Hearts and Minds, 1962.

Tumin, Melvin M. (Editor). *Race and Intelligence.* Anti-Defamation League, 1963.

Tumin, Melvin M. *Segregation and Desegregation.* A revised edition based on studies from 1959 to 1963. New York, Anti-Defamation League of B'nai B'rith.

Turner, Francis A. (Chairman). *Report of the Committee on Integration,* Part I., "Zoning, Human Relations and Teacher Personnel." New York City Board of Education, February 15, 1963.

Tyson, Cyril. "Open Enrollment: An Assessment." *The Journal of Sociology,* October 1961.

The United States Commission on Civil Rights. *Civil Rights U.S.A.* —*Public Schools, Cities in the North and West,* 1962.

The United States Commission on Civil Rights. *Civil Rights U.S.A.* —*Public Schools, Southern States,* 1962.

Weinberg, Myer (Editor). *Integrated Education.* 1424 North Orleans Street, Chicago 10, Illinois. Selected articles and bibliographical references.

Weiner, Max, and Walter Murray. "Another Look at the Culturally Deprived and Their Levels of Aspiration." *The Journal of Educational Sociology,* March 1963.

Williams, Frederick (Chairman). *Report of the Committee to Study Objectionable Terms.* New York City, Board of Education, September 21, 1961.

Wolff, Max (Issue Editor). "Toward Integration of Northern Schools." *The Journal of Educational Sociology,* February 1963.

Wolff, Max. *Educational Park.* Commonwealth of Puerto Rico, New York City Office, June 1963.

Yeshiva University Graduate School of Education. *Proceedings of the Invitational Conference on Northern School Desegregation: Progress and Problems.* April 29, 1962.

Williams, Frederick (Chairman). Report of the Committee to Study Objectionable Terms, New York City, Board of Education, September 21, 1961.

Wolff, Max (Issue Editor). "Toward Integration of Northern Schools." The Journal of Educational Sociology, February 1963.

Wolff, Max. Educational Park, Commonwealth of Puerto Rico. New York City Office, June 1963.

Yeshiva University Graduate School of Education, Proceedings of the Invitational Conference on Northern School Desegregation Programs and Problems, April 20, 1962.

Participating Organizations

American Jewish Committee
New York Chapter

American Jewish Congress
Metropolitan Council

Anti-Defamation League of B'nai
B'rith
New York Regional Office

Bank Street College of Education

Citizens' Committee for Children
of New York, Inc.

City Commission on Human
Rights of New York, Inc.

Commonwealth of Puerto Rico
Migration Division, Department
of Labor

Division of Teacher Education of
the City University of New
York

Hofstra College

Long Island University

National Association for the Advancement of Colored People

National Scholarship Service and
Fund for Negro Students

New York City Public School
System

New York State Citizens Committee for the Public Schools,
Inc.

New York University

Public Education Association

Teachers College, Columbia University

United Parents Associations

Urban League of Greater New
York

Yeshiva University Graduate
School of Education

Conference and Workshop Personnel

Conference and Work Conference Planning Committee

Minna Alperin
American Jewish Congress

Joyce Austin
Office of the Mayor

Sarah Tennessee Baker
National Association For the Advancement of Colored People

Charles A. Bird
Fordham University

Dan Dodson
New York University

Rosa Estades
Commonwealth of Puerto Rico

113

Violet Edwards
New York State Citizens Committee for the Public Schools

Carl Fields
Morris High School

James W. Fogarty
Community Council of Greater New York

Edmund Gordon
Graduate School of Education
Yeshiva University

Richard M. Graf
Long Island University

Calvin E. Gross
New York City Public Schools

Donald Horton
Bank Street College

Dorothy Daily Jones
New York City Commission on Human Rights

Gordon J. Klopf
Teachers College, Columbia University

Israel Laster
American Jewish Committee

Charles M. Long
Bank Street College

P. Bertrand Phillips
Urban League of Greater New York

Richard L. Plaut, Sr.
National Scholarship Service and Fund for Negro Students

Julian Robinson
National Scholarship Service and Fund for Negro Students

Herbert Rosenbaum
Hofstra College

Lester Rosenthal
Long Island University

Harold Schiff
Anti-Defamation League of B'nai B'rith

Ethel Schwabacher
Urban League of Greater New York

June Shagaloff
National Association for the Advancement of Colored People

Rose Shapiro
Public Education Association

Helen Storen
Queens College

Sally Sullivan
Citizen's Committee for Children of New York

Marion P. White
United Parents Associations of New York City

Frederick H. Williams
Human Relations Unit
Board of Education

Max Wolff
Commonwealth of Puerto Rico

Principal Speakers

Martin Deutsch, Institute for Developmental Studies
Joseph Monserrat, Commonwealth of Puerto Rico
John Niemeyer, Bank Street College of Education
Gertrude Noar, Anti-Defamation League of B'nai B'rith

Dan Thompson, Howard University
Melvin Tumin, Princeton University
Lloyd Richards, reading from selected works by James Baldwin

Participants, Conference May 1 and 2
Teachers College, Columbia University

Thelma Adair
Queens College

Minna Alperin
American Jewish Congress

Regina M. Andrews
Washington Heights Branch,
    New York Public Library

Marion Aron
Bank Street College

L. H. Ashe
United Parents Association

Joyce Austin
Office of the Mayor

Sara T. Baker
National Association for the Ad-
    vancement of Colored People

Hubert P. Beck
City College

Amalia Betanzos
United Parents Associations

Dorothy Bloomfield
Bank Street College

Isidore Bogen
Board of Education

Garda Bowman
National Conference of Christians
    and Jews

Aaron Brown
Board of Education

Mildred A. Brown
Teachers College,
    Columbia University

Bernice D. Brooks
Teachers College,
    Columbia University

Judith Burke
Harlem Youth Opportunities
    Unlimited

Nathan Burnett
Urban League of Greater
    New York

James E. Calkins
Administration and Service Center

Sarah A. Cameron
Board of Education

Marion Clark
Board of Education

Frances Cluger
United Parents Association

Esther Cooke
P.S. 31

Edna Crowley
Board of Education

Robert A. Dentler
Teachers College, Columbia
    University

L. Deutsch

Margaret S. Douglas
Board of Education

Zelda Druce
P.S. 208 Brooklyn
United Parents Association

Robert Edgar
Queens College

Violet Edwards
New York State Citizens Committee for the Public Schools, Inc.

Rosa Estades
Commonwealth of Puerto Rico

Carl Fields
Morris High School

Otis E. Finley, Jr.
National Urban League

Mary Finocchiaro
Hunter College

Mary Fisk
Public Education Association

Florence Flast
United Parents Association

Julius Ford

Hilda Fortune
Urban League of Greater New York

Hardy R. Franklin

Clara M. George

H. H. Giles
New York University

Esther Gollobin

William H. Grayson, Jr.
Brooklyn College

Ethel Greenburg
Anti-Defamation League

Martin Hamburger
New York University

June Moss Handler

Marion Hargraves
Panel of Americans

Yvonne Hau
Commonwealth of Puerto Rico

Barney Hendley
Urban League of Greater New York

Raphael Hendrix

Arthur L. Hillis
Brien McMahon High School

Donald Horton
Bank Street College

Leonard W. Ingraham
Board of Education

Marjoria Davis Ison

Edwina C. Johnson

Thelma Johnson
Harlem Youth Opportunities Unlimited

Theron A. Johnson
Intercultural Relations in Education
State Education Department

Dorothy Daily Jones
New York City Commission on Human Rights

John B. King
Board of Education

Ralph D. King
National Conference of Christians and Jews

Gordon J. Klopf
Teachers College, Columbia University

Murray Kubit
Butchers' Union AFL-CIO

Sylvia Kusiel
American Jewish Congress

Jacob Landers
Board of Education

Phil C. Lange
Teachers College, Columbia
University

Israel A. Laster
American Jewish Committee

Essie Lee
Board of Education

Naomi Levine
American Jewish Congress

Blanche Lewis

Edward S. Lewis
Urban League of Greater
New York

Charles M. Long
Bank Street College

Morris Lounds
Urban League of Greater
New York

Virginia Love
Hunter College
Teachers College, Columbia
University

Barbara MacKenzie
Brooklyn College

Eugene T. Maleska
Board of Education

Betty Manson
United Parents Association

Eunice Matthew
Brooklyn College

Dorothy M. McGeoch
Teachers College, Columbia
University

Kate Miano

United Parents Association
Ernest Minott

Helen Mitchell
New York City
Department of Health

Anna S. Murphy

Carmella Nesi
Board of Education

Estelle Neumann
Board of Education

Norma L. Newmark
Board of Education

Gertrude Noar
Anti-Defamation League

Elizabeth O'Daly
Board of Education

Richard Parrish
United Federation of Teachers

Harry Passow
Teachers College, Columbia
University

P. Bertrand Phillips
Urban League of Greater
New York

Richard L. Plaut, Sr.
National Scholarship Service and
Fund for Negro Students

Richard L. Plaut, Jr.
Columbia University School
of Engineering

Victoria Powell

Ruby Puryear
Harlem Youth Opportunities
Unlimited

Ralph S. Rosas
Council of Puerto Rican & Spanish American Organizations

Herbert Rosenbaum
Hofstra College

Rose V. Russell
Teachers Union

Carmen Sanquinetti
Junior High School 117

Henry Saltzman
Ford Foundation

Harold Schiff
Anti-Defamation League

E. Terry Schwartz
Bank Street College

Clarence Senior
Board of Education

Albert Shanker
United Federation of Teachers

Charles Shapp
Board of Education

Rufus Shorter
Board of Education

Harold Siegal
United Parents Association

Sidney Simon
Queens College

Mabel Smythe
New Lincoln High School

Emanuel Stachenfeld
Junior High School 278

Nathan Stillman
Yeshiva University

Martha Stodt
Bank Street College

Walter Stolzenthaler
Board of Education

Helen Storen
Queens College

Sioux Nichols Taylor
Upper Manhattan Branch YWCA

Hillery Thorne
Board of Education

Linda Tiger
Harlem Youth Opportunities
   Unlimited

William H. Toles
Queens Urban League of
   Greater New York

Leolive Tucker
National Association for the Advancement of Colored People

Adele B. Tunick
United Parents Association

Francis Turner
Board of Education

Cyril Tyson
Harlem Youth Opportunities
   Unlimited

Miriam Urdang
Queens College

Donald Watkins
Brooklyn College

Marion White
United Parents Association

Doxey Wilkerson
Yeshiva University

Frederick Williams
Board of Education

Livingston Wingate
Domestic Peace Corps

Charlotte B. Winsor
Bank Street College

Max Wolff
Commonwealth of Puerto Rico

Lillian M. Wornan

Anson W. Wright
State Commission of
Human Rights

J. Wayne Wrightstone
Board of Education

Participants, Work Conference June 14
Bank Street College of Education

Minna Alperin
American Jewish Congress

Regina M. Andrews
Washington Heights Branch,
New York Public Library

Sara Tennessee Baker
National Association for the Advancement of Colored People

Bernice D. Brooks
Teachers College, Columbia
University

Mildred Brown
Teachers College,
Columbia University

Judith Burke
Harlem Youth Opportunities
Unlimited

Esther R. Clay
Urban League of Greater
New York

Robert B. Davis, Jr.
Bank Street College

Robert W. Edgar
Queens College

Rosa Estades
Commonwealth of Puerto Rico

Carl Fields
Morris High School

Florence Flast
United Parents Association

Clara M. George

Esther Gollobin
Lower East Side Neighborhood
Association

Rosa Graham
Bank Street College

Ethel Greenburg
New York City Youth Board

Gladys Harburger
Panel of Americans

Yvonne Hau
Commonwealth of Puerto Rico

Richard Hope
Harlem Youth Opportunities
Unlimited

Donald Horton
Bank Street College

Thelma Johnson
Harlem Youth Opportunities
Unlimited

Dorothy Daily Jones
New York City Commission on
Human Rights

Gordon J. Klopf
Teachers College, Columbia
University

Jacob Landers
Higher Horizons

Israel A. Laster
American Jewish Committee

Essie E. Lee
Board of Education

Blanche Lewis
United Parents Association

Charles M. Long
Bank Street College

Barbara MacKenzie
Brooklyn College

Betty Manson
United Parents Association

Ernest Minott
United Parents Association

Helen Mitchell
New York City
    Department of Health

Joseph Morales
Commonwealth of Puerto Rico

James W. Morrison
Urban League of Greater
    New York

R. Abby Nachman
Teachers College,
    Columbia University

Carmella Nesi
Board of Education

John J. Niemeyer
Bank Street College

Elizabeth O'Daly
Board of Education

M. A. Padilla
Commonwealth of Puerto Rico

Alice Perlman
New York State Citizens Com-
    mittee for Public Schools

P. Bertrand Phillips
Urban League of Greater
    New York

Richard L. Plaut, Sr.
National Scholarship Service and
    Fund for Negro Students

Ralph S. Rosas
Commonwealth of Puerto Rico

Lester Rosenthal
Long Island University

Harold Schiff
Anti-Defamation League of
    B'nai B'rith

Ethel Schwabacher
Urban League of Greater
    New York

Albert Shanker
United Federation of Teachers,
    AFL-CIO

Charles M. Shapp
Board of Education

Harold Siegel
United Parents Association

Emanuel Stachenfeld
Junior High School 278

Sioux Nichols Taylor
Upper Manhattan Branch,
    Young Women's Christian
    Association

Hillery Thorne
Board of Education

Linda Tiger
Harlem Youth Opportunities
    Unlimited

Don Watkins
Brooklyn College

Doxey Wilkerson
Yeshiva University

Max Wolff
Commonwealth of Puerto Rico

Guiding Principles for Securing
Racial Balance in Public Schools

(Statement Proposed by the State Education Commissioner's Advisory Committee on Human Relations and Community Tensions)

In contemporary America, race or color is unfortunately associated with status distinctions among groups of human beings. The public schools reflect this larger social fact in that the proportion of Negroes and whites in a given school is often associated with the status of the school. The educational quality and performance to be expected from that school are frequently expressed in terms of the racial complexion and general status assigned to the school. It is well recognized that in most cases a school enrolling a large proportion of Negro students is viewed as a lower status school. It is also true, of course, that an all white school enrolling a substantial proportion of children from culturally deprived homes is frequently considered less desirable.

A cardinal principle, therefore, in the effective desegregation of a public school system is that all of the schools which comprise that system should have an equitable distribution of the various ethnic and cultural groups in the municipality or the school district. Where serious imbalance exists the school with the highest proportion of minority group and lower-status children tends to receive more of such children as parents who are able to do so move to neighborhoods and schools of higher status.

A program which seeks an equitable distribution of majority and minority group children in all of the schools of a district offers several advantages. It will enable all children to profit from acquaintance with others of different backgrounds than their own, it will reduce distinctions among schools based on noneducational factors, and will probably stabilize the shifts of enrollment which often follow the arrival of minority group children in disproportionate numbers in a particular school.

121

The Committee recognizes that long established patterns and community customs are not easily or quickly changed and that psychological and social factors operate on all sides of such a situation as the one now before you. We therefore suggest six principles which seem to us relevant to the whole question of racial balance in the schools.

(1) The common school has long been viewed as a basic social instrument in attaining our traditional American goals of equal opportunity and personal fulfillment. The presence in a single school of children from varied racial, cultural, socio-economic, and religious backgrounds is an important element in the preparation of young people for active participation in the social and political affairs of our democracy.

(2) In forming school policies, every educationally sound action should be taken to assure not only passive tolerance but active acceptance of and genuine respect for children from every segment of the community, with particular attention given to those from minority groups that may have been the objects of discriminatory mistreatment.

(3) No action, direct or indirect, overt or covert, to exclude any child or group of children from a public school because of ethnic, racial, religious, or other educationally irrelevant reasons should be taken by any public agency. Wherever such action has occurred it is the obligation of the school authorities to correct it as quickly as possible.

(4) No action should be taken which implies that any school or any group of pupils is socially inferior or superior to another, or which suggests that schoolmates of one group are to be preferred to schoolmates of another. In establishing school attendance areas one of the objectives should be to create in each school, a student body that will represent as nearly as possible a cross-section of the population of the entire school district, but with due consideration also for other important educational criteria including such practical matters as the distance children must travel from home to school.

(5) A "neighborhood school" offers important educational values which should not be overlooked. The relation between a school and a definable community with which it is identified can, in many cases, lead to more effective participation by parents and

other citizens in the support and guidance of the schools. It can stimulate sound concern for the welfare of the school and its pupils and can lead to beneficial communication between the school staff and the community that staff serves.

(6) When a "neighborhood school" becomes improperly exclusive in fact or in spirit, when it is viewed as being reserved for certain community groups, or when its effect is to create or continue a ghetto-type situation it does not serve the purposes of democratic education.

June 17, 1963

other citizens in the support and guidance of the schools. It can stimulate sound concern for the welfare of the school and its pupils and can lead to beneficial communication between the school staff and the community that staff serves.

(e) When a "neighborhood school" becomes improperly exclusive in fact or in spirit, when it is viewed as being reserved for certain community groups, or when its effect is to create or continue a ghetto-type situation it does not serve the purposes of democratic education.

June 17, 1963

Responsibilities of the Schools in Integration

Statement of Policy
Board of Education
New York City Public Schools

It has been said, correctly, that the schools alone cannot eliminate prejudice, discrimination, and segregation. It is equally true that this task will not be accomplished with less than an all out effort of the schools.

Our schools must not be neutral in the struggle of society to better itself. We must not overlook the harmful effects of discrimination on the education of all children. Moreover, within the limits of our control, we must not acquiesce in the undemocratic school patterns which are a concomitant of segregated housing. Furthermore, we must continue our policy of not tolerating racial or religious prejudice on the part of any member of our staffs. If education is to fulfill its responsibility, it must recognize that the school world has a significant influence on each child's attitudes and affects the future of democracy.

To further its integration policy, the school system has responsibilities to its pupils and personnel and to the communities.

(1) *For pupils*—We must seek ways to give every child an optimum opportunity for fulfillment and success:

(a) Our school system must vigorously employ every means at its disposal to desegregate schools and classrooms and to bring about true integration as soon as possible.

(b) We must continue to develop educational programs which prepare all pupils to live constructively in a pluralistic society.

(c) We must provide whatever services and materials are essential to meet the special educational needs of those pupils whose progress has been impaired by an accumulation of the ills of discrimination. Simultaneously we must lift the goals of those whose environment has kept their aspirational levels at a low plane.

125

(2) *For School Personnel*—We must develop personnel practices which will maximize the success of the integration program:

(a) We must provide appropriate education and training for school personnel so that every staff member may gain an appreciation of the strengths inherent in the variety of backgrounds that compose our total population.

(b) In recognition of the value to the children of association with professionals of different backgrounds, our staffing procedures must provide for better ethnic heterogeneity in school faculties.

(c) It is essential that capable and experienced teachers and supervisors be distributed in accordance with educational needs.

(3) *With Communities*—We must work closely and cooperatively with communities:

(a) We must support the efforts of those communities which are struggling to overcome past frustration and failure and to surmount present deprivation.

(b) We consider it our obligation to help develop the kind of community attitudes which will help in the implementation of the integration policies of the City public schools.

May, 1963